The Changing Politics
of Federal Grants

LAWRENCE D. BROWN
JAMES W. FOSSETT
KENNETH T. PALMER

The Changing Politics of Federal Grants

THE BROOKINGS INSTITUTION
Washington, D.C.

Copyright © 1984 by
THE BROOKINGS INSTITUTION
1775 Massachusetts Avenue, N.W., Washington D.C. 20036

Library of Congress Cataloging in Publication data:
Main entry under title:
The changing politics of federal grants.
  Includes bibliographical references and index.
  1. Grants-in-aid—United States—Addresses, essays,
lectures.   I. Brown, Lawrence D. (Lawrence D.), 1947–
II. Fossett, James W.   III. Palmer, Kenneth T.
HJ275.C46 1984   336.1'85   84-45275
ISBN 0-8157-1168-9
ISBN 0-8157-1167-0 (pbk.)

9 8 7 6 5 4 3 2 1

THE BROOKINGS INSTITUTION is an independent organization devoted to nonpartisan research, education, and publication in economics, government, foreign policy, and the social sciences generally. Its principal purposes are to aid in the development of sound public policies and to promote public understanding of issues of national importance.

The Institution was founded on December 8, 1927, to merge the activities of the Institute for Government Research, founded in 1916, the Institute of Economics, founded in 1922, and the Robert Brookings Graduate School of Economics and Government, founded in 1924.

The Board of Trustees is responsible for the general administration of the Institution, while the immediate direction of the policies, program, and staff is vested in the President, assisted by an advisory committee of the officers and staff. The by-laws of the Institution state: "It is the function of the Trustees to make possible the conduct of scientific research, and publication, under the most favorable conditions, and to safeguard the independence of the research staff in the pursuit of their studies and in the publication of the results of such studies. It is not a part of their function to determine, control, or influence the conduct of particular investigations or the conclusions reached."

The President bears final responsibility for the decision to publish a manuscript as a Brookings book. In reaching his judgment on the competence, accuracy, and objectivity of each study, the President is advised by the director of the appropriate research program and weighs the views of a panel of expert outside readers who report to him in confidence on the quality of the work. Publication of a work signifies that it is deemed a competent treatment worthy of public consideration but does not imply endorsement of conclusions or recommendations.

The Institution maintains its position of neutrality on issues of public policy in order to safeguard the intellectual freedom of the staff. Hence interpretations or conclusions in Brookings publications should be understood to be solely those of the authors and should not be attributed to the Institution, to its trustees, officers, or other staff members, or to the organizations that support its research.

Foreword

THIS volume takes a broad look at what has happened to federal grants-in-aid since the administration of Lyndon B. Johnson. It discusses the explosive growth of federal aid in the late 1960s and early 1970s; the increase in the share of federal aid going to local governments as opposed to the states; and the efforts of successive presidents since Johnson to rationalize the grant-in-aid system and reduce federal controls.

These studies mark a final chapter in the major research effort carried out by the Brookings Governmental Studies program to evaluate the distributional, fiscal, programmatic, and political effects of general revenue sharing and other broad-based forms of aid that were introduced between 1972 and 1974. Under the direction of Richard P. Nathan, then a senior fellow in Governmental Studies, a national network of experienced social scientists gathered field data on common sets of issues, and a central staff at Brookings aggregated and synthesized the data to highlight national patterns in a series of publications.

The essay on the politics of dependence by James W. Fossett, formerly a research assistant at Brookings and now a staff member of the Institute of Government and Public Affairs and the Department of Political Science at the University of Illinois, is derived directly from the field network research. It synthesizes a series of case studies of the impact of grants-in-aid on selected big cities. The other two essays—by Kenneth T. Palmer on the evolution of grant programs and Lawrence D. Brown on the politics of devolution—were written specially for this volume. Palmer, professor of political science at the University of Maine at Orono, participated in the Brookings network as a field research associate. Brown, associate professor of medical care organization at the University of Michigan, was a senior fellow in the Brookings Governmental Studies program.

The authors acknowledge with thanks the thoughtful review and critical comments of Martha Derthick, who, as director of Governmental Studies from 1978 to 1983, supervised the preparation of these papers for publication. They also thank the several readers who offered comments on various drafts of the essays; Diane Hodges, who gave administrative support to the project; Nancy Davidson, who edited the manuscript; and Ward & Silvan, who prepared the index.

The Ford Foundation largely financed this volume as well as the studies of general revenue sharing with which the field network research began. The research on the impact of grants on big cities that is presented in Fossett's essay was financed by the U.S. Departments of Labor and Commerce. The Brookings Institution is deeply grateful to these funding sources for helping to sustain a large volume of work encompassing a significant period in the history of U.S. intergovernmental relations. The views expressed in this volume are those of the authors and should not be ascribed to the Ford Foundation, the U.S. government, or the trustees, officers, or other staff members of the Brookings Institution.

BRUCE K. MACLAURY
President

April 1984
Washington, D.C.

Contents

Richard P. Nathan and Martha Derthick
Introduction   1

Kenneth T. Palmer
The Evolution of Grant Policies   5

The Johnson Years, 1965–69 6
The Republican Years, 1969–77 21
The Carter Years, 1977–81 35
Reagan's First Two Years, 1981–83 46
Conclusion 51

Lawrence D. Brown
The Politics of Devolution in Nixon's New Federalism   54

The Normative Context 59
Values: Successes and Failures 67
Structure: Successes and Failures 77
Strategy: Successes and Failures 93
The Unstable Politics of Devolution in the Post-Nixon Years 98

James W. Fossett
The Politics of Dependence: Federal Aid to Big Cities   108

Current Ways of Measuring Dependence 110
Redefining Dependence 111
Budgetary and Political Context 114
Explaining Grant Politics 124
The Consequences of Differences in Dependence 139
Conclusion 152
The Consequences of Cuts 153

Index   165

Tables

Kenneth T. Palmer

1. Functional Changes in Federal Aid Outlays, Fiscal Years 1965 and 1969   8
2. Federal Aid Outlays to Urban Areas, by Function, Fiscal Years 1964 and 1969   15
3. Revenue Sources of Special Districts, Fiscal Years 1962, 1967, and 1972   16
4. Outlays for Federal Broad-Based Grants and Other Grants, Fiscal Years 1972 and 1977   29
5. Revenue Sources of Counties, Fiscal Years 1967, 1972, and 1977   29
6. Functional Changes in Federal Aid Outlays, Fiscal Years 1969 and 1977   32
7. Functional Changes in Federal Aid Outlays, Fiscal Years 1977 and 1981   44
8. Functional Changes in Federal Aid Outlays, Fiscal Years 1981 and 1983   48

James W. Fossett

1. Population, Urban Conditions, and Economic Growth in Case Study Cities   119
2. Federal Aid by Type, Fiscal Year 1978   122
3. Three Measures of Dependence on Federal Funds, 1978   124
4. General Fund Revenue Excess or Deficiency as Percentage of General Fund Expenditures, 1973–78   128
5. General Fund Surplus or Deficit as Percentage of General Fund Expenditures, 1973–78   129
6. Cities' Use of Federal Operating Funds for Basic Services, by Financial Condition   140
7. Estimated Percentage of Federal Grant Expenditures Benefiting Low- and Moderate-Income Groups, 1978   148

RICHARD P. NATHAN and MARTHA DERTHICK

Introduction

FEDERAL GRANTS-IN-AID to state and local governments have become so prominent a feature of American government that every national administration must make decisions about their design and use. No president can escape choices about the extent of the federal government's use of grants-in-aid, the allocation of grants among governmental functions and among levels of subnational government, the character and specificity of conditions to be attached to grants, and the level of administrative effort to be spent on enforcing such conditions.

The papers collected in this volume describe the choices recent administrations have made in respect to grant-in-aid policies; analyze why certain of their choices (but not others) have prevailed in American politics; and explain how some of the most important of these choices—in particular, the infusion of large amounts of federal aid into the cities under both Republican and Democratic presidents in the 1970s—have affected the way local governments function.

We hope that these analyses will help to bring about more informed choices of federal grant-in-aid policies and will encourage students of American federalism to pursue research on the consequences of different policies. In the past, choices of grant policies and intergovernmental policies in general have usually been guided by inherited doctrines—that is, beliefs about where authority and power ought to lie in the federal system in order to maximize certain values; partisan strategies that seek to take advantage of, or consciously to alter, the distribution of partisan influence in the federal system; or tactical calculations of what is required to advance a particular favored measure or policy goal. To these familiar raw materials of policy choice we would like to add more and better information, derived from empirical research, about the actual implications of different choices.

In the 1970s the Governmental Studies program of the Brookings Institution mounted a major effort at research on the consequences of some of the most important innovations in grant-in-aid policies, especially the introduction of general revenue sharing in 1972. Several volumes of findings have already appeared; they cover, in addition to general revenue sharing, public service employment grants, the community development block grant program, and the combined impact of grant programs in several major cities.[1] This volume is one more result of that broad effort, but whereas previous publications have focused on particular grant-in-aid programs or jurisdictions, this one seeks to take a more comprehensive look at what has happened in the grant-in-aid system as a whole.

Kenneth T. Palmer's essay covers the major steps in the evolution of grants-in-aid since the Johnson administration. Besides tracing the volume of expenditures—which grew explosively under Johnson, Nixon, and Ford, rose more slowly under Carter, and then fell under Reagan—Palmer analyzes shifts in the functional allocation of grant spending, the level and type of subnational units favored as recipients, and the amount of federal supervision that accompanied grants. He finds some partisan continuities. All of the Republican presidents have pursued devolution, but whereas for Nixon and Ford this meant giving more aid *and* more discretion to state and local governments, Reagan has sought to return some functions altogether to the states while reducing aid, a more radical approach to grants consistent with his overriding desire to curtail federal expenditures. The grant policies of Democratic administrations have been marked above all by a concern for alleviating economic and social distress. Under Johnson this concern was manifested in the proliferation of grants for health, education, and manpower training; under Carter, in a less profligate decade, it was manifested in an effort to "target" aid to the big cities, the principal concentrations of poverty. However, Palmer detects no consistent partisan positions with respect to the level of government—states or localities—to

1. Richard P. Nathan and others, *Monitoring Revenue Sharing* (Brookings Institution, 1975); Richard P. Nathan, Charles F. Adams, Jr., and associates, *Revenue Sharing: The Second Round* (Brookings Institution, 1977); Richard P. Nathan and others, *Public Service Employment: A Field Evaluation* (Brookings Institution, 1981); Paul R. Dommel and associates, *Decentralizing Urban Policy: Case Studies in Community Development* (Brookings Institution, 1982); Charles J. Orlebeke, *Federal Aid to Chicago* (Brookings Institution, 1983); Thomas J. Anton, *Federal Aid to Detroit* (Brookings Institution, 1983); Susan A. MacManus, *Federal Aid to Houston* (Brookings Institution, 1983); Henry J. Schmandt, George D. Wendel, and E. Allan Tomey, *Federal Aid to St. Louis* (Brookings Institution, 1983); and Sarah F. Liebschutz, *Federal Aid to Rochester* (Brookings Institution, 1984).

be preferred as the recipient of aid, and he argues that the proliferation of grants in the late 1960s caused presidents of both parties to be very much concerned with issues of management and control—what Lawrence D. Brown elsewhere has called "rationalizing " policies.[2]

Lawrence D. Brown's essay deals with devolution because it is the single most significant contemporary innovation in grant policies and mainly with the Nixon administration's proposals for general and special revenue sharing because they are the leading examples of devolution whose fate can be analyzed from observation and experience. Brown seeks to explain the success of some devolution measures and the failure of others by reference to three variables: values, defined as normative views on the desirable and proper workings of government; structure, meaning the more or less stable relationships within and among institutions, including both public ones and private ones that seek to influence public policy; and strategy, meaning those discrete elements of policy that politicians may manipulate in hopes of building a coalition adequate to win enactment of a proposal. He concludes that the devolution triumphs of 1972–74, which included general revenue sharing and block grants for manpower programs and community development, were limited and circumstantial innovations, not first decisive steps down the road to comprehensive reform of the grant-in-aid system.

James W. Fossett's essay focuses on the cities because they have been the principal beneficiaries of devolution and of the massive expansion of federal grants that took place in the 1970s. He asks to what extent large cities have become dependent on the federal government as a source of revenue, and he argues that the answer depends on how a city uses the aid, which in turn depends more than anything else on the city's fiscal condition, the amount of discretion it has in using federal funds, and the level of political organization among the beneficiaries of federal programs. Cities with major financial problems, considerable discretion in the use of federal dollars, and well-organized political systems are more likely than other cities to have become financially dependent on federal dollars, in the sense that they use substantial amounts of such funds to support basic city services.

To be truly comprehensive and to analyze the politics of all grant programs at all levels of government would be a monumental task. The

2. Lawrence D. Brown, *New Policies, New Politics: Government's Response to Government's Growth* (Brookings Institution, 1983).

central challenge of empirical research on grants lies in the extreme complexity of the subject: the bewildering array of programs and governments compels selectivity, which puts generalizations at risk.

The work done at Brookings in the past decade sought to meet the methodological challenge by gathering data on the impact of grants from a sample of state and local jurisdictions through a network of field associates—persons trained as social scientists who were knowledgeable about local affairs and who collaborated with a central staff at Brookings in the preparation of research designs. In this way, research at different locations was guided by a common framework, making it possible for analysts on the central staff to interpret and synthesize the findings.[3] Fossett's essay, which is based on case studies of major cities done by Brookings field associates, is such a synthesis and contrasts the impact of federal grants in different jurisdictions.[4]

The other two essays also depend importantly on comparisons, though of a different kind. Palmer's method in describing the evolution of grant policies at the national level is to contrast the approaches of different presidents and their administrations, while Brown, in order to understand the politics of devolution, contrasts different clusters of programs.

We believe that the various comparative frameworks illustrated here will prove helpful to future analysts of grant policies as they seek to comprehend the seemingly endless series of national initiatives and state and local responses. The turbulence portrayed in all of these essays shows no sign of coming to an end. The Reagan administration continues to devise offers of freedom from federal controls in exchange for lowered state and local expectations of federal funding, its version of devolution. And, no matter what bargains in intergovernmental relations may be struck by Ronald Reagan, successors in pursuit of different policy goals will surely attempt to renegotiate them.

3. For an extended discussion of the method, see Richard P. Nathan, "The Methodology for Field Network Evaluation Studies," in Walter Williams and others, *Studying Implementation: Methodological and Administrative Issues* (Chatham House, 1982), pp. 73–99.

4. His essay here is a revised version of his book, *Federal Aid to Big Cities: The Politics of Dependence* (Brookings Institution, 1983).

KENNETH T. PALMER

The Evolution
of Grant Policies

FEDERAL AID to state and local governments expanded massively during the administrations of Lyndon B. Johnson, Richard M. Nixon, Gerald R. Ford, and Jimmy Carter. All of these presidents chose to rely heavily on grants to achieve their domestic purposes. However, they made different choices with respect to the functional areas that were given priority, the latitude allowed states and cities in the use of federal funds, and the type of subnational governments given preference as recipients.

The purpose of this essay is to provide a compact history of the major trends in grant-in-aid policies since 1965. The essay demonstrates that, even as aid dollars constantly expanded, each administration had a distinctive impact on the grant system as a whole. The discussion reflects the chief concerns of each administration and the modifications in federal assistance it tried to bring about: the Johnson presidency's greatly expanded use of categorical grants to address social problems; the Nixon-Ford presidencies' pursuit of devolution under the concepts of the New Federalism; and the Carter administration's efforts to redesign federal grants to "target" aid to needy localities. A brief, and more tentative, discussion of the Reagan administration presents the continuities and contrasts between the Reagan grant policies, as they have evolved thus far, and those of preceding administrations.

The author gratefully acknowledges the research assistance of University of Maine (Orono) students Kenneth D. Hodgkins, Stephen H. Holden, Rebecca A. Cayford, Leona M. Coulombe, Deborah M. Franz, and Scott A. Shanley in the several drafts of this paper. He also thanks Janice E. Palmer and Veria M. Poling for their typing assistance and the staff of the Government Documents Department of the Fogler Library of the University of Maine at Orono.

The Johnson Years, 1965–69

The year 1965 marked a watershed in the history of federal grants. Lyndon Johnson took office as an elected president, and with the backing of large Democratic majorities in both houses of the Eighty-ninth Congress, produced new legislation in health, housing, manpower training, education, urban planning, and many other fields. It was the most productive congressional session since the 1930s, and most of the legislative initiatives took the form of grants-in-aid to states and communities. In just two years the Eighty-ninth Congress increased the number of separate grant-in-aid authorizations from 221 to 379.[1] A substantial impact on state and local budgets was felt almost immediately. Over a period of two years (1965–67) federal grants to states and cities rose from 18.8 to 20.7 percent of domestic federal expenditures and from 14.8 to 16.9 percent of the total revenues of subnational governments.[2]

Although federal grants-in-aid were a well-established feature of the U.S. government, they had historically been confined to a few specific areas. As late as 1965 the two major functional categories receiving assistance, transportation (highways) and income security (public assistance), together accounted for about two-thirds of all federal aid dollars. The effect of the work of the Eighty-ninth Congress was to diffuse grants-in-aid throughout the domestic functions. When it adjourned, nearly all traditional state and local governmental activities were receiving some federal assistance. By 1969 the proportion of federal aid dollars assigned to highways and public assistance had accordingly decreased to one-third of a much-expanded aid package.

Functional Growth

The basis upon which Johnson sought expansion of grant programs was his vision of the Great Society. First expounded in a speech at Ann Arbor, Michigan, in 1964, Johnson's Great Society encompassed at least two distinct ideas. One was to improve the quality of American life. As the

1. Advisory Commission on Intergovernmental Relations, *Fiscal Balance in the American Federal System*, vol. I (Washington, D.C.: ACIR, 1967), p. 151.
2. *Special Analyses, Budget of the United States Government, Fiscal Year 1969* (Government Printing Office, 1968), p. 161.

president described it in his 1965 State of the Union message: "The Great Society asks not how much, but how good; not only how to create wealth but how to use it; not only how fast we are going, but where we are headed."[3] He asked for legislation to end the pollution of air and water and to control and prevent crime and promised to launch "a national effort to make the American city a better and a more stimulating place to live."

The other Great Society concept involved raising the floor under people's living standards and in particular providing new forms of federal assistance to disadvantaged persons who were not able to benefit from existing programs. The president stated that a "basic task" was "to open for all Americans the opportunity that is now enjoyed by most Americans." In furtherance of that goal, he proposed to begin "a program in education to ensure every American child the fullest development of his mind and skills . . . [and] a massive attack on crippling and killing diseases."[4] These programs in particular envisioned both major new spending commitments and more complex federal-state-local relationships.

Under the Johnson administration, the total amount of aid disbursed to states and localities nearly doubled between 1965 and 1969. The greatest increases were concentrated in the area of social welfare, where the rate of growth was about twice that for all grants (see table 1). New legislation in the health, education, and manpower fields accounted in particular for that increase.

HEALTH

One landmark piece of Great Society legislation, passed in 1965, created medicaid to help the states care for medically indigent persons. Before 1965 the federal government provided grants-in-aid to the states to assist only the medically indigent aged, a program authorized by the Kerr-Mills Act in 1960 as a compromise forerunner of medicare. In 1965 Congress adopted medicare to finance health care for the elderly, making it part of the social security system and thus independent of grants-in-aid, but the grant-in-aid approach, under the name of medicaid, was now applied to all persons who were either receiving public assistance (in federally aided categories) or who were medically indigent but not on welfare. Under medicaid, the federal government contributed between 50 and 83 percent of the state's costs, depending on the state's per capita income.

3. *Public Papers of the Presidents of the United States: Lyndon B. Johnson, 1965* (GPO, 1966), p. 4. (Hereafter *Public Papers: Johnson, 1965.*)

4. Ibid., p. 5.

Table 1. *Functional Changes in Federal Aid Outlays, Fiscal Years
1965 and 1969*

| | 1965 | | 1969 | |
Function	Amount (millions of dollars)	Percentage of total	Amount (millions of dollars)	Percentage of total
Defense and international affairs, veterans	46	0.4	61	0.3
Agriculture	518	4.8	807	4.0
Natural resources	223	2.0	518	2.6
Commerce and transportation	4,386	40.2	4,710	23.3
Housing and community development	559	5.1	1,670	8.2
Education, health, welfare, manpower (excluding public assistance)	2,301	21.1	8,542	42.2
Public assistance	2,787	25.6	3,652	18.0
Energy	. . .	. . .	. . .	. . .
Law enforcement	. . .	. . .	28	0.1
General government aid	84	0.8	267	1.3
Total	10,904	100.0	20,255	100.0

Source: *Special Analyses, Budget of the United States Government, Fiscal Years 1967, 1971.* Figures are rounded.

Medicaid greatly increased the numbers of persons eligible for federal assistance to help defray medical expenses, and federal spending rose rapidly in the first years of the program. In 1966 the federal government contributed $975 million of the approximately $2 billion spent on medical assistance for needy persons; by fiscal 1969 grants to the states for medical assistance reached nearly $2.3 billion.[5]

EDUCATION

The most significant education measure in the Great Society program was the Elementary and Secondary Education Act (ESEA) of 1965. This act provided, for the first time, general federal support for public elementary and secondary schools. The ESEA had a controversial gestation, its passage hindered during the Kennedy administration by congressional conflicts over aid to church-related schools. Johnson's strategy was to focus the

5. General information on legislation in this paper has been drawn from the *Congressional Quarterly Almanac*, vols. 21–38, and *Congress and the Nation*, vols. 1–5 (Congressional Quarterly, 1965–82). Information on grant outlays has been drawn from *Special Analyses, Budget of the United States Government, Fiscal Years 1967–1985*.

measure on assistance to low-income school districts across the nation.[6] In such districts both public and private schools might obtain the benefit of some federal aid. The ESEA was passed with wide support in the Senate, although a majority of Republicans in the House opposed it. Title I of the act, which provided approximately $1 billion, was designed to provide assistance to school districts with impoverished children. The law contained a formula under which the number of children from low-income families was multiplied by one-half of each state's average expenditure per school child. To qualify for aid, a school district needed to have only 3 percent of its children in low-income families; districts in some 95 percent of U.S. counties were eligible. The largest concentration of funds went to inner-city schools in the North and to rural districts in the South. In 1966, title I was amended to allow a state to use the national average expenditure per school child (instead of its own average expenditure) in calculating dollar assistance; this change further benefited the poorer states. Within each school district, federal funds under title I could be used for a variety of purposes, so long as impoverished children were aided and state and federal agencies approved of local spending plans.

Other portions of the ESEA provided assistance to states for school libraries and textbooks. Title III encouraged states to experiment with innovative programs, including educational centers that provided services that individual schools might lack. Most grants under this title were made directly from the U.S. Office of Education to local school agencies, which applied for the funds. Amendments to the ESEA after 1965 continued to focus on the needs of the disadvantaged. In 1966 funds were made available to the states for the education of mentally and physically handicapped children. In 1967 new assistance was approved for the education of children from non-English-speaking families and for the prevention of school drop-outs.

MANPOWER LEGISLATION

The effort to meet the needs of disadvantaged persons also characterized the Johnson administration's manpower programs. The level of unemployment was relatively low during the Johnson administration (generally under 4 percent). However, the favorable economic conditions highlighted the persistent unemployment problems of certain groups, such as youth,

6. See Stephen K. Bailey and Edith K. Mosher, *ESEA: The Office of Education Administers a Law* (Syracuse University Press, 1968), chap. 2.

among whom joblessness was much higher than that for all workers. The Johnson administration generally moved away from attempts to correct cyclical unemployment and unemployment in specific regions of the country—notably Appalachia, in which the Kennedy administration had taken a particular interest—and instead moved to attack structural unemployment (caused by lack of skills or education) on a national basis—an effort that involved major new aid programs for state and local governments in the manpower field.

The stress on assisting the hard-core unemployed began with the Economic Opportunity Act of 1964, which contained a number of new categorical programs.[7] The Job Corps focused on training disadvantaged youths between the ages of sixteen and twenty-one in residential centers. The Neighborhood Youth Corps provided part-time work experience to young persons still in high school who appeared likely to be dropouts. Other programs addressed the needs of older workers in rural areas and sought to train disadvantaged young adults to become paraprofessionals in health and social service fields. Two long-standing aid programs, vocational education and vocational rehabilitation, were modified during the Great Society so that their funds could be spent on larger groups of needy persons. Within vocational education, Congress ordered that particular attention be paid to handicapped persons, which it defined in both physical and economic terms. Amendments to the Vocational Rehabilitation Act in 1965 brought the mentally handicapped into the program (it had been limited to the physically impaired). In 1968 a further broadening occurred when the category of "socioeconomic disadvantaged" was included under the act. Federal grants for major vocational education and rehabilitation and manpower training activities in state and local governments accordingly rose rapidly, from about $300 million in 1965 to about $1.1 billion in 1969.

NUTRITIONAL PROGRAMS

During the 1960s considerable attention was focused on the incidence of hunger and malnutrition in the United States. Some estimates at that time indicated that as many as 10 million persons suffered from malnutrition. To address this problem, the Johnson administration established on a permanent basis a food stamp plan that had been tried experimentally during the Kennedy administration. In 1966 it won approval of new leg-

7. Richard P. Nathan and others, *Monitoring the Public Service Employment Program*, vol. 2 (National Commission for Manpower Policy, March 1978), chap. 1.

islation to create a school breakfast program for children from low-income families. Two years later, in 1968, the administration successfully supported legislation expanding food service programs established under the National School Lunch Act of 1946 to needy children located in settlement houses, centers for the handicapped, playgrounds, day care centers, and other facilities as well as in schools. Grants for nutritional programs approximately doubled (from about $300 million to slightly less than $600 million) in the 1965–69 period.

New federal spending on grant-in-aid programs in education, manpower, health, and welfare (excluding public assistance) accounted for $6.24 billion of the $9.35 billion increase in aid spending between 1965 and 1969 (see table 1). Taken together, these program areas underwent a nearly fourfold rise in federal aid during that period.

Urban Emphasis

In his 1965 State of the Union address, President Johnson promised that the problems of cities would receive a high priority in the building of the Great Society. Urban areas soon became the focal point of the administration's intergovernmental policy. Two months later the president sent a special message to Congress on the nation's cities, affirming that in the quest for an improved quality of life, "the future of the American city will play the most vital role."[8]

The administration's urban policies had two principal dimensions. One was to adjust categorical grants in some program areas to respond more directly than before to the needs of cities. For example, the Hill-Burton Act, originally passed in 1946, was revised by Congress in 1964 to permit improvement of urban hospitals as well as construction in rural areas and small towns. The other part of the Johnson urban policy was to design new legislation or refashion existing legislation to meet the peculiar problems of large cities.

THE DEPARTMENT OF HOUSING AND URBAN DEVELOPMENT

In 1965 the administration won approval in Congress for a new Department of Housing and Urban Development (HUD).[9] President Kennedy

8. *Public Papers: Johnson, 1965*, p. 240.

9. See Judith H. Parris, "Congress Rejects the President's Urban Department, 1961–62," in Frederick N. Cleaveland and associates, *Congress and Urban Problems: A Casebook on the Legislative Process* (Brookings Institution, 1969), pp. 173–223.

had proposed such a department in 1961 after campaigning for the idea in
1960, when it was part of the Democratic party platform. During the
Kennedy administration the proposed department encountered various
difficulties in Congress. Some resistance was due to the widely held belief
that Robert Weaver, a black who was then head of the Housing and Home
Finance Agency, would be the secretary of the new department. The main
problem, however, seemed to be that northern liberal Democrats, who
were the strongest supporters of the proposal, did not have a working
majority in either house.

President Johnson endorsed the department measure after he succeeded
Kennedy in 1963, but Congress did not vote again on the bill until 1965,
after the 1964 elections had enlarged the Democrats' majority, mostly with
liberals who could be expected to support the new department. Additionally, some modest changes in the bill helped win support from three
interest groups that had earlier been opposed—the National Association
of Counties, the U.S. Savings and Loan League, and the National Association of Home Builders. These changes gave greater authority to the
secretary and assigned housing matters a more prominent place in the
department structure.

The House passed the bill by a margin of 217 to 184; the Senate, by 57
to 33. Republicans continued to oppose the idea, but Democratic majorities
were now large and cohesive. The creation of the Department of Housing
and Urban Development was a recognition of the need for a sustained
effort in Washington to deal with the problems of the nation's cities.

HOUSING

A significant part of the Johnson administration's urban policy consisted
of two large pieces of housing legislation. The Housing and Urban Development Act of 1965 authorized nearly $8 billion in grants over a four-year
period to underwrite programs and set out some new directions in federal
housing policy. The act tried to establish a closer link between housing
and urban renewal programs. The Housing Act of 1949 had had the dual
purpose of encouraging slum clearance and providing low-income housing.
But in practice the two were rarely linked. Between 1949 and 1965, once
urban renewal sites were cleared of slums, they typically were redeveloped
for commercial, industrial, or high-income residential purposes. In the
1965 act, Congress permitted one-third of the urban renewal funds to be
used for nonresidential purposes, but it required that in residential projects
the city "provide a substantial number of units of standard housing of low

and moderate cost and result in marked progress in serving the poor and disadvantaged people living in slum and blighted areas."[10] A second measure, enacted in 1968, strengthened that effort by stipulating that a majority of all housing units had to be made available to low- and moderate-income persons, and that at least 20 percent of the units had to be designed for low-income families. The 1968 legislation extended the housing program to areas outside the urban renewal projects in order to slow the deterioration of declining neighborhoods awaiting urban renewal. In trying to overcome the socially segregating effects of previous public housing and urban renewal programs, the Johnson administration also greatly expanded payments to individuals for housing assistance. The 1965 measure contained a rent-supplement provision for those who could not secure adequate rental housing for 25 percent of their income; the 1968 legislation provided for low-interest loans to encourage home ownership. A key goal in each case was to enable economically disadvantaged families in urban areas to live outside of public housing projects.

MODEL CITIES

The most innovative Great Society measure affecting cities was the Demonstration Cities and Metropolitan Development Act of 1966, which embodied a new strategy of grants-in-aid. A Task Force on Urban Problems appointed by Johnson in 1965 criticized existing federal aid programs as "too small and too diffused to have guided the process of urban development," and "too much oriented to specific functions."[11] As an alternative the task force recommended concentrating and coordinating resources, including federal assistance funds, on particular areas within cities. The objectives would be "to completely eliminate blight in the designated area and to replace it with attractive, economic shelter" and to effect "a change in the total environment of the area affected, with ample provision of public facilities: schools, hospitals, parks, playgrounds, and community centers."[12]

The key to the program consisted of grants to participating cities equal to 80 percent of each city's matching contribution for other federal grants used in a demonstration area. The city had considerable discretion in using such funds. It might employ them to defray its local contribution for the

10. National Commission on Urban Problems, *Building the American City* (Praeger, 1969), p. 157.
11. Charles M. Haar, *Between the Idea and the Reality* (Little, Brown, 1975), pp. 293–94.
12. Ibid., p. 296.

other federal grants, such as ones for urban renewal or code enforcement, or it might undertake projects not federally aided but needed by the city, such as improving refuse collection or equipping playgrounds. While cities of all sizes were invited to apply for assistance, Congress required that HUD follow numerous criteria in awarding grants. A city had to show that the problems in a demonstration area warranted a comprehensive renewal effort, that projects undertaken would help reduce ill health and unemployment and increase low- and moderate-cost housing, and that the implementation of projects would involve widespread citizen participation. Some sixty-three cities were awarded planning grants by late 1967, including all but one of the U.S. cities with a population of over 1,000,000 and eight cities with populations under 20,000.[13] Congress authorized about $1 billion for the program in its first three years.

The demonstration cities bill (or model cities bill, as it came to be called shortly after its passage) embodied some important premises about the structure of city governments. An earlier federal strategy to help cities coordinate federally aided social programs had emerged in 1964, when Congress and the president declared a war on poverty and created the Office of Economic Opportunity (OEO) to wage that war. Under the OEO, the agencies of coordination at the local level—called community action agencies (CAAs)—were obliged by both the Economic Opportunity Act of 1964 and instructions from the OEO to enlist the participation of the residents of the neighborhoods served. Some CAAs were predominantly composed of program beneficiaries; in a number of cities, the CAA worked in strenuous opposition to city hall. To the extent that they became instruments of political combat, CAAs proved to be poor instruments for the coordination of federal programs in their communities. Mindful of this problem, HUD officials specified that the operating agency under model cities ("the city demonstration agency") should be "closely related to the governmental decision-making process in a way that permits the exercise of leadership by responsible elected officials."[14] The new emphasis was on using a city's own political leaders, elected on a citywide basis, to help tie together federal aid programs.

As table 2 indicates, creation of new urban-oriented programs under the Great Society, and the redefinition and reauthorization of some existing programs, led to increases in the level of federal assistance for cities at a

13. Ibid., p. 145.
14. James L. Sundquist, *Making Federalism Work* (Brookings Institution, 1969), p. 83.

Table 2. *Federal Aid Outlays to Urban Areas, by Function,*
Fiscal Years 1964 and 1969
Millions of dollars unless otherwise indicated

Function	1964	1969	Percentage increase 1964–69
Agriculture and rural development	271	417	53.9
Natural resources and environment	18	180	900.0
Commerce and transportation	2,147	2,539	18.3
Community development and housing	348	1,610	362.6
Education and manpower	732	2,963	304.8
Health	300	2,278	659.3
Income security	1,695	3,899	130.0
General government and defense	77	159	106.5
Total for urban areas	5,588	14,045	151.3
Total federal aid outlays	10,141	20,255	99.7
Percentage of total federal aid outlays to urban areas	55.1	69.3	...

Source: *Special Analyses, Fiscal Year 1971.* Figures are rounded.

rate five times greater than increases in funds for nonurban areas. Put
differently, federal aid for cities rose one and one-half times faster than
did federal assistance generally. The Great Society years marked a time
when urban areas *first* received from the federal government a level of
assistance approximately proportionate to their population. While the shift
in policy was led by President Johnson and Democratic leaders in Congress,
both congressional parties appeared to support it.

The Design of Federal Grants

The huge increase in the number of grant-in-aid authorizations in the
early years of the Great Society was accompanied by some changes in grant
design. One important modification was a growing use of grants to pursue
distinctively national goals. Until the 1960s, federal assistance programs
were mostly designed to help states and their subdivisions carry out their
own traditional functions, such as building roads and providing public
health services and support for the dependent poor. In the 1960s, federal
aid programs began to set forth national objectives and to enlist subnational
governments in carrying out these national goals, rather than the other
way around. This change was reflected in the language of certain major

Table 3. *Revenue Sources of Special Districts, Fiscal Years*
1962, 1967, and 1972[a]

Millions of dollars unless otherwise indicated

Revenue source	1962	1967	Percentage increase 1962–67	1972	Percentage increase 1967–72
Intergovernmental revenue	376	635	68.9	1,550	144.1
Federal government	159	244	53.5	808	231.1
State government	57	152	166.7	205	34.9
Local government	160	239	49.4	538	125.1
Own-source revenue	1,405	2,102	49.6	3,679	75.0
Total general revenue	1,781	2,737	53.7	5,229	91.0

Source: U.S. Bureau of the Census, *1962 Census of Governments; 1967; 1972*. Figures are rounded.
a. Does not include school districts.

statutes. For example, the Demonstration Cities and Metropolitan Development Act of 1966 asserted that "Congress hereby finds and declares
that improving the quality of urban life is the most critical domestic problem
facing the United States."[15] The proclaiming of national goals was fully
consistent with the themes of the Great Society, which was by definition
one society to be created on a national scale.

The use of subnational governments by the federal government to pursue
national objectives led to an increased federal involvement with local-level
special districts. Among the various types of governments, special districts
were considered attractive to a grant-in-aid policy that used subnational
governmental units as way stations for the attainment of national objectives
and packaged its funds in specific program categories. A special district
typically performed only one or two governmental functions, such as
providing water, maintaining a hospital, or operating an airport. As table
3 notes, the growth of federal aid dollars for special districts was especially
rapid in the years 1967–72 when many Great Society measures were fully
implemented.

Acting consistently with its pursuit of national goals, the federal government in 1965–69 greatly expanded its use of "project grants," which
give more discretion to federal administrators than do "formula grants,"
which flow automatically to recipient governments in accordance with
statutory criteria. Of the 158 grant authorizations added in 1965 and 1966,
some 130 (or 82 percent) were project grants. Because project grants are

15. Ibid., p. 4.

awarded competitively among applicants, decisionmaking on grant funding centers in the federal bureaucracy; thus the rise in project grants contributed to an increase in federal power over state and local affairs. Congressional reliance on project grants also comported well with the urban emphasis of the Great Society. The use of these subventions enabled the federal government to provide financial aid directly to cities at a time when the data to construct federal grant formulas for city programs had not been fully developed.

CONTROVERSY

When the Johnson administration took office, federal funds were directed almost entirely to the states, and aid dollars were funneled into delimited program categories that permitted little discretion over their use by recipient governments. After 1965 the proliferation of categorical grant programs and the bypassing of the states for a broad and sometimes ill-defined array of purposes threw intergovernmental relations into confusion. A principal difficulty was that "in the enactment of the new programs of federal assistance, scant attention was paid to the pattern of federal-state-local relations that was emerging."[16] Presidential and congressional concern tended to focus on the goals of new programs, rather than on the administrative arrangements under which they were to be carried out. Intergovernmental coordination emerged as a major problem by the midpart of the Great Society period. In early 1966, Senator Edmund S. Muskie, Democrat of Maine, chairman of the Senate Subcommittee on Intergovernmental Relations, reported to the Senate on a study his unit had made of the issue:

We found substantial competing and overlapping of Federal programs, sometimes as a direct result of legislation and sometimes as a result of empire building. Similar competition and duplication were found at the State and local levels. We learned that too many Federal aid officials are not interested in, and in fact are even hostile to coordinating programs within and between departments, and that they are reluctant to encourage coordination and planning at State and local levels. These conditions frequently and predictably result in confusion and conflicting requirements which discourage State and local participation, and adversely affect the administrative structure and fiscal organization in these jurisdictions.[17]

The issues of coordination tended to focus on the amount of flexibility recipient governments should have in using federal aid dollars.

16. Ibid., p. 13.
17. Ibid., p. 15.

President Johnson himself articulated no particular philosophy concerning the form federal assistance should take. Although he made some gestures suggesting he perceived a need for a more flexible grant system for state and local officials, he seemed basically committed to the categorical grant arrangement. The stimulus for modification of categorical grants came mainly from the Republican party. Following the 1966 elections, in which the Republicans gained forty-seven new seats in the House, the question of categorical grants versus block grants developed as a major congressional issue. Representative Melvin Laird, Republican of Wisconsin, listed some of the problems with the categorical system:

the lack of adequate resources at the Federal level . . . needed to do an effective job in all of the areas in which the Federal Government operates. . . . the reluctance of this administration in particular to set any meaningful priorities among its hundreds of programs. . . . [the failure] to realize . . . that a general solution devised in Washington may very well help the situation in Milwaukee, but that the same solution may compound the problem in New York.[18]

Republican spokesmen generally favored the increased level of federal grant funds, but preferred that localities have more discretion over their use. As one party position paper expressed it: "Instead of grants for hundreds of different programs, and thousands of projects, Federal funds to State and local governments could be allocated to a few broad functional areas such as education, welfare, health, highways, etc., with decisions as to the exact applications of the funds left to the recipient governments."[19]

THE PARTNERSHIP FOR HEALTH ACT

The first block grant ever enacted was the Partnership for Health Act of 1966. The passage of this measure provoked little controversy compared to later block grants. The reason was that the bill was mainly perceived as technical corrective legislation.[20] In 1935 Congress had enacted the Public Health Act, which provided for a general grant to the states for health services. In succeeding years, as new health problems emerged, Congress provided specific categorical grants in such areas as cancer control, mental health, and crippled children's services. By 1966 the general health grant that thirty years earlier had accounted for 100 percent of state-directed federal health funds now represented only 6 percent of federal assistance

18. *Congressional Record* (February 15, 1967), pp. 3447, 3449.
19. Ibid. (April 10, 1967), p. 8817.
20. Advisory Commission on Intergovernmental Relations, *The Partnership for Health Act: Lessons from a Pioneering Block Grant* (Washington, D.C.: ACIR, 1977), chap. 2.

for health services. A number of groups, including a 1965 White House Conference on Health, argued that comprehensiveness could be achieved only if state officials had more flexibility in the administration of health funds.

President Johnson supported the partnership bill. In a message to Congress in March 1966, he noted that meeting the health needs of "the individual and his family, living in their own community . . . demands coordinated use of all the resources available."[21]

As enacted, the measure replaced nine formula grant programs with a single block grant for comprehensive health services. However, the act contained a special provision for mental health services, requiring that 15 percent of the block grant funds go to the state's mental health agency. Funding for the act was slightly higher than it had been for the separate categorical programs; that the block grant entailed no major increase or decrease in funding contributed toward muting congressional conflict over the new arrangement.

THE SAFE STREETS ACT

A more controversial measure was the Omnibus Crime Control and Safe Streets Act of 1968. Recognizing that crime rates were rising, especially in urban areas, President Johnson stated in 1967 that law enforcement was now a national problem and recommended legislative action. He called for a categorical assistance program for local governments, funded at $50 million in the first year and $300 million in its second year. Eligible communities had to have populations over 50,000. For several reasons the president's proposal encountered considerable congressional opposition.[22] First, unlike the Partnership for Health Act, this proposal would bring the federal government into a new policy area that was traditionally the province of state and local government. A second problem was that in law enforcement the governmental level with the greatest responsibility had usually been local government, whereas the states had traditionally been the recipients of federal aid and arguably were the appropriate recipient from a constitutional point of view. A third dilemma was the matter of categorical grants versus block grants. Some federal guidance was clearly necessary to ensure proper use of federal funds, but communities around the country

21. *Health and Education Message from the President of the United States*, H. Doc. 89-395, 89 Cong. 2 sess. (GPO, 1966), p. 3.

22. Advisory Commission on Intergovernmental Relations, *Safe Streets Reconsidered: The Block Grant Experience 1968–1975* (Washington, D.C.: ACIR, 1977), chap. 2.

just as clearly needed discretion in combating different types of law enforcement problems.

Introduced first into the House, the administration bill moved through the Judiciary Committee largely unscathed, but a major change was made on the House floor. Under an amendment proposed by Representative William Cahill, Republican of New Jersey, and supported by a coalition of Republicans and Southern Democrats, the law enforcement assistance measure was transformed from a categorical grant for localities into a block grant for states. State planning agencies created by the governor would be the initial recipients of funds. The amendment included a pass-through provision that required that the majority of the funds go to localities, but under state supervision. Proponents of the amendment argued that the administration's approach gave the U.S. attorney general too much power over thousands of U.S. localities and might lead to creation of a national police force.

In the Senate, the block grant amendment was deleted in committee, but later reinstated after a floor fight led by the Republican minority leader, Senator Everett Dirksen of Illinois. Dirksen argued that the president's approach was "a circumvention of constitutional policy against Federal controls over State and local police powers."[23] He also argued that because local police departments were so numerous, state planning and coordination were necessary to make the program successful. As finally passed, the Safe Streets Act created a block grant, with funds allocated to the states on a formula basis according to population. Some 75 percent of the operating funds were to pass through to local governments.

THE ELEMENTARY AND SECONDARY EDUCATION ACT

The question of state versus local planning was also an issue in the reauthorization of the Elementary and Secondary Education Act in 1967. In the House, Republicans attempted to make the act into a block grant for the states. They maintained that the U.S. Office of Education had too much authority under the arrangement adopted in 1965, which provided federal aid directly to localities. Democrats countered that some state education departments, if equipped with block grant money, would not treat urban areas fairly in subsequent allocations. A Republican block grant amendment failed when Southern Democrats, many of whose districts were receiving substantial funding under the ESEA's title I, refused to

23. *Congressional Record* (May 23, 1968), p. 14753.

join in the effort. However, in a subsequent battle, Republican House members were successful in transforming title III of the ESEA, dealing with supplementary educational services and centers, into a block grant to be administered by state education departments.

The Republican Years, 1969–77

The political controversy surrounding the design of federal grants, which erupted in the law enforcement and education programs, persisted after those issues were settled. The upshot of the continuing battle was the emergence of the New Federalism of the Nixon-Ford administrations. The New Federalism offered an alternative to the Great Society in defining the "proper" role of the federal government in relation to state and local governments. Under Nixon, issues of federalism, especially those relating to the design of grants, reached a high point of conceptualization, and important changes followed. The allocation of funds among functions—an important issue during the Johnson years—received relatively little attention. Federal aid continued to grow, both as a proportion of the federal budget and as a share of state and local spending, though the yearly rate of increase was not quite so rapid as it had been in the four Great Society years.

The New Federalism: Origins and Aims

Unlike the Johnson administration, the Nixon administration did not have an explicit urban policy. Its policy toward large cities was part of a more general approach, the New Federalism, which shaped its actions toward all subnational governments. While the New Federalism was a program of a Republican administration, its beginnings rested in complaints about the federal grant system voiced by politicians across the political spectrum. As one observer put it, "A period of . . . extraordinary effort at social improvement . . . concluded in a miasma, some would say a maelstrom, of social dissatisfaction."[24] Dissatisfaction seemed to center around two problems generally related to the Great Society programs. One was the proliferation of grant authorizations. The Great Society had launched

24. Daniel P. Moynihan, "Policy vs. Program in the '70s," *The Public Interest*, no. 20 (Summer 1970), p. 90.

remedies for the various social ills it sought to cure in the form of separate grant authorizations for individual programs. Each program was the responsibility of a particular agency, bureau, or department in the federal bureaucracy. By the late 1960s the fragmentation of grants had produced much overlap and duplication, causing state and city officials to be confused about what programs were available to them and which federal officials they should be working with.

Another problem was that the proliferation of categorical programs and the pursuit of nationally defined social goals inescapably brought about a large amount of federal influence in local affairs. Some programs implied a significant redistribution of local power and in some big cities the threat of federally sponsored social turbulence as well. The citizen participation requirements attached to the community action program of the War on Poverty proved especially controversial. As a result, politicians from both parties, though employing different rhetoric, joined in attacks on the federal establishment in 1968. Campaigning in Utah for the Democratic presidential nomination, Robert Kennedy maintained that "we must return control to the people themselves," since "in the last analysis it should be in the cities and towns and villages where the decisions are made, not in Washington."[25] Richard M. Nixon, shortly before his nomination, declared that "if we persist in treating complex local needs from remote centers, we'll be repeating tomorrow mistakes that have added dangerously to the frictions of today."[26]

While dissatisfaction with the federal bureaucracy was a pervasive theme in 1968, a different general idea expressed in that election year sounded a more positive note: state and local governments were effective providers of public services and could be trusted to do independently some of the work that federal agencies were attempting to direct and supervise. This was mainly a Republican position. In the immediate post–New Deal period, Republicans generally opposed enlargement of federal activity, even in the form of categorical grants, and preferred instead tax cuts that would return money to individuals; by the late 1960s, however, they had acquired some recognition of the positive role that states and communities might play. In 1958 Representative Laird introduced the first revenue-sharing measure in the House of Representatives. The Laird proposal would have returned to each state 5 percent of its federal income taxes and reduced

25. *New York Times*, March 28, 1968.
26. Ibid., June 28, 1968.

by an equivalent amount the state's share of federal categorical funds for health, welfare, and education. Republican platforms in 1960 and 1964 called for major revisions in the grant-in-aid system with the goal of enhancing the responsibilities of the states. State government budgets and staffs during that period were expanding rapidly. Between 1950 and 1967 the states nearly quadrupled their expenditures (from $11 billion to $40 billion) and more than doubled their number of employees (from 1.1 million to 2.3 million).[27] In his 1968 campaign, Nixon stressed that governmental activism at the subnational level now needed recognition from Washington. He explained his approach in terms of a revenue or tax-sharing plan:

The whole point of a tax sharing program is to take advantage of both the Federal Government's power and efficiency as a tax collector and state and local governments' efficiency and effectiveness as problem solvers. But if we are to truly gain the latter advantage, then we cannot make the Federal directives too specific lest we tie the hands of administrators at the local level.[28]

THE NEW FEDERALISM PROPOSALS

In a speech to the nation on August 8, 1969, President Nixon described the elements of what he called the New Federalism. He presented a package of four legislative ideas that he said offered "a new and drastically different approach to the way in which government cares for those in need, and to the way the responsibilities are shared between the State and the Federal Government."[29]

The president first proposed replacement of the existing program of aid to families with dependent children with a federally administered program called the family assistance plan. Benefits under the AFDC had always varied widely among the states (in 1969, according to Nixon, the monthly range was from $39 to $263 for a family of four). The president recommended that the federal government guarantee a significantly higher minimum benefit level (for a family of four, the proposed yearly figure was $1,600), which could be supplemented by the states. His second proposal was to overhaul manpower training programs and consolidate them into packages that would be administered primarily by state and local governments and hence "be better adapted to specific state and local needs." The third proposal was to restructure the Office of Economic Opportunity, admin-

27. Kenneth T. Palmer, *State Politics in the United States* (St. Martin's Press, 1972), chap. 1.
28. *New York Times*, October 27, 1968.
29. *Public Papers: Nixon, 1969*, p. 638.

istrator of the War on Poverty, so as to give most of its functions to established cabinet departments and limit it to experimental programs as "a laboratory agency." Nixon's final proposal was for federal revenue sharing with states and communities, to begin in the middle of fiscal 1971 at a cost for that year of $500 million.

The *New York Times* referred to the president's program as an "Ideological Mixmaster," "a baffling blend of Republicanism and radicalism."[30] While the president sought to decentralize one program (manpower), and to provide new aid to state and local governments in another (revenue sharing), he had spoken of centralizing welfare responsibilities in the federal government. Still, the several parts of the Nixon program did seem to reflect some key underlying ideas that had developed as critiques of the Great Society initiatives.[31]

The fundamental premise of the New Federalism was the need to sort out the appropriate activities of each level of government. Nixon suggested that not all governments should be involved heavily in all policy areas. Rather, the national government should concentrate on what it did best— transferring income, primarily—whereas subnational units should provide services, such as manpower training, community redevelopment, and protecting public health. A second concept of the New Federalism was that the role of generalist officials, such as governors, legislators, mayors, and city managers, should be strengthened and made central in the management of intergovernmental aid programs.

SORTING OUT FUNCTIONS

Besides making cash welfare payments principally a responsibility of the federal government, the Nixon administration would have further consolidated the food stamp and unemployment compensation programs in the hands of federal agencies, consistent with its preference for making income transfers predominantly a federal function. Also deemed appropriate to the federal government was any activity that entailed large spillover effects. Thus Nixon during his first term pressed for various new federal controls and grants in environmental protection. A third area of activity judged to be national in character was demonstrations and research. None-

30. *New York Times*, August 17, 1969.
31. For a fuller discussion of the ideas of the New Federalism, see "The Publius Symposium on the Future of American Federalism," *Publius*, vol. 2 (Spring 1972), pp. 95–146. Also see Richard P. Nathan, *The Plot That Failed: Nixon and the Administrative Presidency* (Wiley, 1975), especially chap. 2.

theless, in the sorting out of governmental activities, the New Federalism was thought of mainly as an effort to devolve responsibilities to states and cities.

The Johnson administration had ended any doubt about the demise of dual federalism, namely, the idea that the functions of the states and the federal government could be partitioned neatly into separate spheres. The New Federalism presumed that the federal government should continue to be involved in financing most programs, even when policymaking and administration were under the authority of state and local government.[32] Federal financing, however, would depend on a subnational government's willingness to operate within broad federally set requirements, such as civil rights standards. Further, devolution would apply only to certain programs. The prime candidates were activities that a government itself managed (as distinct from income maintenance programs, which involved a transfer of money from some citizens to other citizens via government). Domestic programs that the Nixon administration sought to devolve included community development, transportation, and manpower training. In these policy arenas local needs differed, and substantial program discretion for local officials therefore seemed appropriate.

GENERALISTS VERSUS SPECIALISTS

In the realm of structure, Nixon's New Federalism emphasized general-purpose governments as the appropriate recipients of federal aid. This meant both that it did not experiment with so-called paragovernments— that is, semipublic agencies created for the purpose of receiving federal funds, such as community action agencies and neighborhood organizations—and that it sought to enhance the role of generalist officials, especially elected ones, rather than functional specialists. An example of the Nixon efforts here was the chief executive review and comment program, begun in 1971, under which chief executives in selected large cities were empowered to review all applications for federal funds emanating from their jurisdictions, including applications from nonprofit organizations and agencies legally separate from the chief executive's office. The program appeared to help about half the participating cities in coordinating federal programs in their boundaries.[33]

An effort to decentralize and to reassign authority within the federal

32. "The Publius Symposium," pp. 132–37.

33. Advisory Commission on Intergovernmental Relations, *Improving Federal Grants Management* (GPO, 1977), chap. 5.

bureaucracy complemented the emphasis on devolution to generalist state and local officials. The president tried to move decisionmaking power over many categorical grants from Washington to federal regional offices. In March 1969 Nixon ordered the establishment of uniform regional boundaries and common regional headquarters for five federal departments (previously, most departments had their own regional office networks). Within a year, additional departments had located their offices in the ten cities selected as sites for federal regional headquarters. In March 1969 the president also created federal regional councils in these cities, comprised of representatives of the major federal departments, to work with states and localities.[34] Each council was chaired by a representative of the Office of Management and Budget. Additionally, the Nixon administration tried to strengthen the office of the regional director, a generalist official, in federal departments, and to have this official work closely with governors and mayors on categorical grant programs.

The Design of Federal Grants

Under the Republicans' New Federalism, the pursuit of distinctive national goals was relaxed in favor of state and local discretion. The centerpiece of the New Federalism was revenue sharing, authorized by the State and Local Fiscal Assistance Act of 1972. Before long, it was complemented by the passage of two block grants, the Housing and Community Development Act of 1974 and the Comprehensive Employment and Training Act of 1973.

THE STATE AND LOCAL FISCAL ASSISTANCE ACT

The Nixon administration's revenue-sharing measure, although proposed in 1969, was not enacted until three years later. It was also considerably modified. The administration proposed that funds be divided between states and localities on an approximate 50–50 basis. However, Congress adopted a House Ways and Means Committee recommendation that two-thirds of revenue-sharing funds go to localities and one-third to the states. The Ways and Means Committee chairman, Representative Wilbur Mills, Democrat of Arkansas, who was instrumental in making the

34. See Martha Derthick, *Between State and Nation: Regional Organizations of the United States* (Brookings Institution, 1974), chap. 7. Regional councils were started on an experimental basis in four cities in 1968 during the Johnson administration.

change, argued that the fiscal problems of localities were more acute than those of the states.[35] Additionally, the public interest organizations of state and local officials that had formed a coalition to lobby for revenue sharing tended to be weighted toward localities.

The initial appropriation for revenue sharing was $30.2 billion, allocated among some 38,000 general-purpose governments over a five-year period. While the allocation formulas took account of tax effort and poverty factors, perhaps the most notable feature of the program was inclusivity, and hence dispersion of funds: all subnational general-purpose governments were made part of the federal aid system for the first time.

THE HOUSING AND COMMUNITY DEVELOPMENT ACT

The Housing and Community Development Act, the largest block grant enacted during the Nixon-Ford period, was a watershed in the development of federal grant programs directly aiding cities. The act consolidated seven previously established categorical programs for urban areas, including urban renewal, model cities, water and sewer facilities, open spaces, neighborhood facilities, rehabilitation loans, and public facility loans. Some $8.45 billion was authorized for the first three years of the program.[36] Funds were allocated on a formula basis. Communities had to submit an application to HUD, but the agency's discretion to deny an application was limited. HUD had to act within seventy-five days (otherwise an application was automatically approved) and could refuse funding only if a city's planned activities were "clearly not permissible" under the act or "clearly inconsistent" with the city's stated needs. About 3,000 localities received funds in 1975, approximately half of which had received no HUD funds previously. The act required no matching funds from recipient communities.

THE COMPREHENSIVE EMPLOYMENT AND TRAINING ACT

Like the Housing and Community Development Act, the Comprehensive Employment and Training Act of 1973 (CETA) sought to enlarge the discretion of state and local officials.[37] Title I of CETA contained a single-formula grant to states and localities to enable them to operate a variety

35. Richard P. Nathan and others, *Monitoring Revenue Sharing* (Brookings Institution, 1975), pp. 361–65.
36. Richard P. Nathan and others, *Block Grants for Community Development* (U.S. Department of Housing and Urban Development, January 1977), p. 51.
37. Nathan and others, *Monitoring the Public Service Employment Program*, chap. 1.

of manpower activities such as job counseling, placement, training, and work experience. In the Johnson years, separate categorical grants existed for most of these functions, and most projects were subject to approval by the Department of Labor. Under CETA, day-to-day administration of manpower programs was in the hands of prime sponsors, which were cities and counties of 100,000 or more population. States were eligible as prime sponsors for areas not covered by local governments. Prime sponsors were required to submit plans to the Department of Labor for approval, but otherwise they had considerable discretion in setting goals and implementing the program. Other titles authorized the secretary of labor to provide grants for public service jobs in areas of high unemployment and to provide special manpower assistance for various categories of persons with particular needs or disadvantages. Congress provided approximately $2.4 billion in 1975 for CETA programs.

Not all of the Nixon administration's proposals for block grants were passed by Congress. In 1971 the president had recommended six block grant (what he called "special revenue-sharing") programs to Congress for urban community development, rural community development, education, manpower training, law enforcement, and transportation. Only the urban development and manpower proposals were enacted. The education and transportation grant consolidations met resistance in Congress and were buried in committee. Some of what the administration wanted in its rural development proposal was included in the Rural Development Act of 1972. The changes recommended in law enforcement were modest alterations in an already-existing block grant; these were partially included in the Crime Control Act of 1973, but the proposal was the least important of the six. Still, two major block grants were set in motion, and, together with revenue sharing, they significantly increased the proportion of all federal assistance made up of broad-based aids. As table 4 indicates, during 1972–77 such assistance grew from about one-tenth of all federal dollars disbursed to subnational governments to about one-quarter of the total aid package.

The subnational governments that benefited from the broad-based assistance were, of course, general-purpose governments. During the Johnson administration federal aid to local governments grew most rapidly for special districts, but in the Republican years the largest increases in federal aid went to county governments. As table 5 shows, the dollar level of federal assistance for counties increased nearly ten times between 1972 and 1977. Federal grants accounted for less than 2 percent of county general

Table 4. *Outlays for Federal Broad-Based Grants and Other Grants, Fiscal Years 1972 and 1977*

Millions of dollars unless otherwise indicated

	1972		1977	
Type of grant	Amount	Percentage of total	Amount	Percentage of total
Broad-based grants[a]	3,419	9.9	17,865	26.1
Other grants[b]	30,953	90.1	50,531	73.9

Source: *Special Analyses, Fiscal Year 1979*. Figures are rounded.
a. Includes general-purpose grants, such as revenue sharing, and various block grants.
b. Primarily categorical grants.

Table 5. *Revenue Sources of Counties, Fiscal Years 1967, 1972, and 1977*

Millions of dollars unless otherwise indicated

Revenue source	1967	1972	Percentage increase 1967–72	1977	Percentage increase 1972–77
Intergovernmental revenue	5,020	9,956	98.3	18,816	89.0
Federal government	158	405	156.3	3,738	823.0
State government	4,694	9,252	97.1	14,347	55.1
Other	168	299	78.0	731	144.5
Own-source revenue	7,451	13,696	83.8	22,746	66.1
Total revenue	12,472	23,652	89.6	41,562	75.7

Source: U.S. Bureau of the Census, *1967 Census of Governments; 1972; 1977*. Figures are rounded.

revenues in 1972; by 1977 counties were depending on federal assistance for some 9 percent of their revenues. The most immediate cause of the increase was the federal revenue-sharing program enacted in 1972. As general-purpose governments, counties shared in this program; special districts, which did not participate in revenue sharing, found their level of federal assistance increasing at a proportionately slower rate in 1972–77 than in 1967–72. Another factor contributing to the much-expanded federal support for counties was the movement by many urban counties into such federally aided activities as housing, environmental protection, health, and manpower training. In some states counties began to take over parts of these functions from financially hard-pressed central cities, and they usually secured assistance from federal programs.

FORD AND THE NEW FEDERALISM

Though President Gerald R. Ford as Nixon's successor supported most of the ideas of New Federalism, he was primarily concerned with devolution in the form of block grants to states and cities. In 1976, in his State of the Union address and in his budget message, Ford moved to put his own stamp on grant policies by proposing four new block grants—a health grant that would have included medicaid, an education block grant similar in content to Nixon's recommendation, a child nutrition block grant, and a grant for social services for the needy. In urging support for his four grant proposals, Ford pointed often to the community development block grant as the appropriate model for federal-local relationships. Speaking in Chicago to a group of newspaper editors a few weeks after his State of the Union address, the president observed:

Up until 1974, we had seven different categorical grant programs for urban development. . . . When we did away with the seven . . . grant programs and turned it into a community development program, one allocation to a community, we reduced the number of forms significantly. We have reduced the number of Federal employees significantly, and we have reduced the burden on the local units of government in a meaningful way. If we could do it in that program, I see no reason why we cannot do it in the other four programs that I have mentioned.[38]

None of Ford's recommendations won approval in Congress.

Several summary points may be made about changes in grant design in the Nixon-Ford period.[39] As noted, grants became distinctly more broad-based, with one-quarter of all federal subventions being in that form by 1977. If transfer programs, such as medicaid, food stamps, and housing assistance, are excluded from the calculation, the proportion of aid in broad-based form in 1977 rises to 39 percent. Consistent with this was the tendency during the 1970s for Congress to enact formula grants, in contrast to the extensive use of project grants in the Johnson years. Between 1967 and 1978, the proportion of categorical grants represented by formula grants moved from 26 percent (99 of 379 programs) to 35 percent (170 of 492 programs). Another trend was that Congress tended to impose lower matching requirements on grant recipients in specific programs. Fifty-one percent of all grant programs in 1975 required a local match of 10 percent or less, compared with 44 percent in 1968. However, because of a relatively

38. *Public Papers: Ford, 1976–77*, p. 660.
39. The material below is based on: Advisory Commission on Intergovernmental Relations, *Categorical Grants: Their Role and Design* (GPO, 1977), chap. 4; Advisory Commission on Intergovernmental Relations, *A Catalog of Federal Grant-in-Aid Programs to State and Local Government: Grants Funded FY 1978*, A-72 (ACIR, February 1979), pp. 1–7; U.S. Bureau of the Census, *Governmental Finances in 1968–69, 1976–77*; and U.S. Bureau of the Census, *City Government Finances in 1968–69, 1976–77*.

high local match required in certain large programs such as medicaid, the overall ratio of federal grant dollars to dollars raised by state and local governments remained fairly constant.

A final basic tendency in the Republican period was dispersal of funds to the benefit of all local governments. In 1968–69 12 percent of federal aid went directly to localities. By 1976–77 this figure had grown to almost 30 percent. Each of the major broad-based grants-in-aid enacted during the Nixon-Ford years—revenue sharing, community development, and CETA—primarily benefited localities, and by the end of the Republican years some 38,000 local governments were regularly receiving federal aid, most for the first time. During the 1970s cities became much more dependent than before on federal assistance. For all cities, the proportion of general revenues represented by federal aid dollars increased from 4.7 percent in 1968–69 to 14.6 percent in 1976–77. For cities having more than 300,000 population, the figures were slightly higher (5.6 percent of their revenues consisted of federal aids in 1968–69; some 15.1 percent did so by 1976–77).

Functional Growth

Concerned mainly with the distribution of aid dollars in support of social policy goals, the Johnson administration had sponsored a huge increase in the volume of social welfare grants. Its urban policy evolved from the broadening of assistance into new program areas, as did changes in the design of grants-in-aid themselves. In the Republican period, by contrast, changes in grant design were the central concern and the distribution of aid dollars across various program areas did not change as dramatically as in the Johnson years.

As table 6 shows, total federal assistance rose from $20.3 billion in 1969 to $68.4 billion in 1977. As a part of domestic federal outlays, assistance dollars moved from 21.3 percent in 1969 to 22.8 percent in 1977, when President Ford left office. Grants-in-aid as a fraction of state and local expenditures rose from 17.4 percent in 1969 to 26.4 percent in 1977. The areas of greatest growth were in programs of social welfare, environmental protection, and general-purpose assistance to subnational government. Increases in these three areas accounted for about four-fifths of the rise in grant-in-aid dollars in the Nixon-Ford period.

Table 6. *Functional Changes in Federal Aid Outlays, Fiscal Years
1969 and 1977*

	1969		1977	
Function	Amount (millions of dollars)	Percentage of total	Amount (millions of dollars)	Percentage of total
Defense and veterans	61	0.3	175	0.3
Agriculture	807	4.0	371	0.5
Natural resources and environment	518	2.6	4,188	6.1
Commerce and transportation	4,710	23.3	8,317	12.2
Community and regional development	1,670	8.2	4,496	6.6
Education, health, welfare, manpower (excluding public assistance)	8,542	42.2	34,119	49.9
Public assistance	3,652	18.0	6,351	9.3
Energy	. . .	. . .	74	0.1
Law enforcement	28	0.1	713	1.0
General government aid	267	1.3	9,592	14.0
Total	20,255	100.0	68,396	100.0

Source: *Special Analyses, Fiscal Years 1971, 1979.* Figures are rounded.

SOCIAL WELFARE

In dollar amounts, the largest growth occurred in the social welfare
area, which had also received the most new funds in the Johnson years.
In percentage terms, however, social welfare did not grow as fast as did
general-purpose aid (new in the 1970s) and environmental assistance (greatly
expanded in the 1970s). Social welfare (excluding public assistance payments) accounted for 50 percent of all federal assistance dollars expended
in 1977, compared with 42 percent in 1969. The main cause of the increase
was the existence of entitlement programs, now growing "uncontrollably."
The leading example was the medicaid program, which grew from $2.3
billion to $9.9 billion in the 1969–77 period. Nutritional programs, for-
mulated in the 1960s to assist needy persons and initially funded at rather
modest levels, were another example. These grants increased nearly sixfold
during the Republican years, from $600 million to $3.4 billion.

Because they incorporate grants only, the public assistance expenditures
in table 6 underestimate the federal government's effort in that field. In
January 1974 public assistance programs for the blind, disabled, and aged

became a direct federal program, known as supplemental security income. Likewise, food stamp benefits became a direct federal program in 1971. Although the family assistance plan failed, the Nixon administration had partially succeeded in its effort to nationalize the income support function. The rise in spending in public assistance categorical grants recorded in table 6 reflects mainly increases in the AFDC program, which remained fundamentally a responsibility of the states, though heavily financed with federal aid.

Federal assistance for manpower training and public service employment grew sharply during the Nixon-Ford years. Unemployment was a serious problem in most of the period and reached a yearly high of 8.5 percent in 1975. In 1971 the Emergency Employment Act authorized a public employment program that was designed to assist areas with unemployment rates of 4.5 percent or more. Funding for this program was $1 billion in 1972 and $1.25 in 1973, but dropped to $250 million in 1974 following the 1973 passage of CETA, which included provisions (title II) aimed primarily at structural unemployment. With a recession growing in 1974, Congress added a new title (title VI) to CETA authorizing some $2.5 billion to employ more than 300,000 persons in community-related services. Generally, Democrats in Congress forced new expenditures for the job-creation measures on the Republican presidents.

Another area of rapid growth was in social services. In 1962 Congress provided funds to help states offer welfare recipients services, such as homemaker and child care services. These grants grew very steeply in the early years of the Nixon administration, from $354 million in 1969 to nearly $1.7 billion in 1972, largely because a loosely written law permitted states to make extensive claims on the Department of Health, Education, and Welfare for aid.[40] In 1972 Congress set a limit of $2.5 billion on this program.

ENVIRONMENTAL ASSISTANCE

In 1972 Congress passed over President Nixon's veto the Federal Water Pollution Control Act Amendments, which set a national goal of eliminating all pollutant discharges into the nation's waters by 1985. The act provided for $18 billion in grants to states for the construction of waste treatment works in 1972–75. The federal government would pay up to 75 percent of

40. See Martha Derthick, *Uncontrollable Spending for Social Services Grants* (Brookings Institution, 1975).

the cost of new plants and make some reimbursements for plants that were constructed or were under construction before 1972. For the rest of the Nixon-Ford period, the waste treatment works grant was one of the largest categorical grants in the federal aid system. It was also one of the few programs established in the Republican years that designated state governments as recipients. However, the operation of the program primarily benefited localities, where the treatment plants were built.

GENERAL AID

The revenue-sharing act, passed in 1972, was renewed in 1976 for three years and nine months (until September 30, 1980), thus moving the program to a fiscal-year basis rather than a calendar-year basis.[41] The federal government was to provide up to $6.85 billion a year to states and communities. The changes made in the original law were fairly modest. Citizen participation and antidiscrimination provisions were strengthened. However, a prohibition against using revenue-sharing funds to match other federal grants and a requirement that revenue dollars should be used for certain priority categories were eliminated. The basic formula for distribution was retained.

In 1976 Congress enacted a new and experimental form of general aid— "countercyclical" grants to communities and states where unemployment was high. The purpose was to incorporate subnational governments in a national policy of economic stabilization. In time of recession the federal government frequently moves to create jobs and to put additional funds into the economy, but states and communities may at the same time counter these actions by laying off employees and raising their own taxes to fight the recession. The theory of countercyclical aid was that states and localities, especially ones hard-pressed by economic downturns, should be provided with adequate funds to prevent layoffs and to enable them to maintain services.

The 1976 measure authorized the secretary of the treasury to make grants up to $1.25 billion over five calendar quarters (ending September 30, 1977) to subnational governments. Quarterly payments were to total $125 million plus $62.5 million for each 0.5 percent increase above 6 percent in the national unemployment rate (for the quarter ending three months earlier). Grants to individual jurisdictions were based on a formula

41. For a discussion, see Richard P. Nathan, Charles F. Adams, Jr., and associates, *Revenue Sharing: The Second Round* (Brookings Institution, 1977).

relating their 1976 revenue-sharing funds to their amount of unemployment over 4.5 percent (localities with less than 4.5 percent unemployment were barred from the program). The grants had to be used to maintain basic services. The measure also provided $2 billion through September 30, 1977, for public works projects. The public works section likewise contained a formula directing funds to those localities hardest hit by unemployment. The legislation was enacted over President Ford's veto. However, it soon turned out to be a key component of President Jimmy Carter's grant policies.

The Carter Years, 1977–81

The Johnson and Nixon-Ford administrations each had a fairly distinct conceptual overview of the intergovernmental system. The two visions differed, of course. While the Great Society stressed the oneness of the federal system, the New Federalism sought to distinguish rather methodically the responsibilities of the national government from those of subnational jurisdictions. The administration of Jimmy Carter seemed not to have as explicit a conception of the federal role in state and local affairs. Carter assumed the presidency under conditions that were clearly less auspicious for the making of bold moves in intergovernmental policy. When Lyndon Johnson and Richard Nixon took office, the unemployment rate was lower than in 1977, and they did not have to face the intense problems of energy shortages and inflation that afflicted the nation when Carter was inaugurated.

Nonetheless, Carter did recommend some technical changes in existing grants, including their formulas. By the late 1970s grants applied so heavily to most areas of state and local activity and their volume was so large that even modest alterations in the design of one or more grant programs could have a major impact on the federal system. In his 1976 campaign Carter had indicated sensitivity to the interests of local governments: to the U.S. Conference of Mayors he had promised he would be "a solid supporter on which you can always depend."[42] In his first month in office he sought revision of certain large grant programs to help localities.

42. *New York Times*, June 30, 1976.

The Design of Grants

A "stimulus package," consisting largely of the reauthorization and
modification of three existing grant programs, was recommended by Carter
to combat poverty and recession at the local level.[43] He asked for a
reauthorization of the countercyclical and public works package of 1976
and an extension and revision of titles II and VI of the Comprehensive
Employment and Training Act of 1973. The thrust of the changes was to
concentrate the programs more intensively on localities especially distressed by unemployment and poverty.

The idea of targeting aid to needy localities was not new with the Carter
administration. Under the Johnson administration, project grants were in
many instances designed to focus on the needs of cities with large numbers
of the poor. However, with the rise of formula grants in the Nixon-Ford
years, federal funds tended to be dispersed among all localities. Smaller
communities gained in proportion to the very large ones, where the heaviest
concentrations of the poor were found. In 1968, 62 percent of all federal
grants for cities went to cities of over 500,000 population; by 1975 only 44
percent went to these large cities. The proportion of assistance for smaller
cities rose accordingly between 1968 and 1975. Communities with populations between 100,000 and 499,999 obtained 18 percent of all federal
grant funds for cities in 1968, but 23 percent in 1975. The proportion of
funds disbursed to communities under 100,000 rose even more sharply,
from 20 percent in 1968 to 33 percent in 1975.[44] President Carter's economic
recovery program was designed to refocus funds on needy areas. As he put
the matter to a group of broadcasters and newspaper editors early in 1977:

> More of all Federal programs, not just a few of them, will be channeled into
> the deteriorating and needy urban downtown areas, whereas in the past they were
> channeled, I think, too much, to the sunbelt area and to the suburbs where the
> need was least.[45]

ELEMENTS OF THE PACKAGE

The most important part of the stimulus package involved countercyclical
assistance. Carter recommended that the countercyclical program of aid

43. Some of the material on the Carter administration is drawn from *Urban Policy Watch*,
vols. 1 and 2 (Washington, D.C.: National Urban Coalition, 1978–79).

44. Richard P. Nathan and Paul R. Dommel, "The Cities," in Joseph A. Pechman, ed.,
Setting National Priorities: The 1978 Budget (Brookings Institution, 1977), p. 295.

45. *Public Papers: Carter*, 1977, p. 949.

to states and localities be extended for five years, with an annual authorization of $2.25 billion. The administration also tried to make the funding more sensitive to changes in the unemployment rate. Congress, however, passed only a one-year extension authorizing a total of up to $2.25 billion ($125 million each quarter when the national unemployment rate reached 6 percent, with additional funds for each 0.1 percent increase above 6 percent).

The second part of the stimulus package was an extension of the public works program that had been enacted in 1976, when Congress had authorized $2 billion for public works projects through September 1977. Under Carter's urging, Congress authorized an additional $4 billion for public works projects through calendar year 1978. Under the formula adopted, 65 percent of the funds was apportioned among the states on the basis of the number of unemployed. The remaining 35 percent was distributed among states with levels of unemployment above 6.5 percent. State governments as such, however, had little involvement in this grant program beyond approving local projects. The Department of Commerce, which administered the program, distributed approximately 95 percent of the funds directly to the localities. State governments received only about 5 percent of the money.

The president's third main proposal was to reauthorize the CETA program, which expired in 1977, and direct it more at the hard-core unemployed. Carter asked that the criteria for individuals' participation in the program be tightened and that the length of participation be shortened. In 1977 Congress extended the program for one year, and in 1978 it accepted most of the president's recommendations. CETA was reextended for four years. The measure provided about 660,000 public service jobs at 1978 unemployment levels. A public service employee was limited to eighteen months of work in any five-year period. For the first time, both income and unemployment requirements were established for eligibility. Participants had to have been recently unemployed and to have come from economically disadvantaged families. The average wage of participants in the program was, with some exceptions, limited to $7,200. Employment was restricted to entry-level jobs, and not less than 10 percent of the funds in fiscal 1979 had to be used for training (this figure was to rise to 22 percent by fiscal 1982). Thus the new CETA measure moved federal funds away from temporary public service employment and toward job training for severely disadvantaged persons. It also tightened requirements on local administration.

REAUTHORIZATION OF THE COMMUNITY DEVELOPMENT ACT

Although it was not part of the stimulus package, the Community Development Act was reauthorized in 1977 and reflected in some new amendments a heightened concern with the targeting of federal funds. The amendments were developed during the Ford administration, but were strongly supported by Carter.

Under the 1974 act, the formula for distributing block grant funds among cities was based on a city's population, overcrowding in housing, and poverty (weighted double). Because of lower wage scales in southern and some western cities, the formula worked to favor cities in those regions— a result that seemed inconsistent with the act's goal of alleviating physical blight in declining cities, most of which were to be found in the Northeast and Midwest.

The Carter amendments called for basing community development funding on age of housing (50 percent), poverty (30 percent), and growth lag (20 percent). The housing variable employed the number of units built before 1940; the growth lag indicator was the extent to which a city's growth rate fell behind the average rate for cities in the 1960–73 period. Of the 259 cities that were projected to benefit under the new formula by 1980, 205 were in the northeast quadrant of the country.[46] Other amendments targeted funds more sharply within cities. The 1974 law had stipulated that communities should give "maximum feasible priority to activities which will benefit low- or moderate-income families." In the 1977 revision, the language was changed to read "low- *and* moderate-income."[47] The amended law also specifically provided for the denial of applications from cities that failed to comply with the income-targeting objectives.

The amendments also authorized urban development action grants (UDAGs) to be used by unusually distressed cities for large-scale development programs. A total of $1.2 billion was authorized for UDAGs for three years beginning in 1978. The secretary of HUD was required to consider levels of distress in awarding grants. HUD's regulations required that projects included in grant applications attract private investment.

The Carter administration's stress on targeting was found in the decisions

46. Paul R. Dommel and others, *Decentralizing Community Development* (U.S. Department of Housing and Urban Development, June 1978), chap. 2. The 1974 formula was also retained in the 1977 revision; cities could choose the formula under which they wished to receive funds.

47. Paul R. Dommel and others, *Targeting Community Development* (U.S. Department of Housing and Urban Development, January 1980), chap. 2.

of federal grant agencies as well as in new provisions of law. In early 1977 HUD Secretary Patricia Harris told a House subcommittee that HUD would "expect communities to direct development and housing programs toward low- and moderate-income citizens." Secretary Harris added, "I do not consider this to be just an objective of the block grant program; it is the highest priority of the program."[48] To carry out that objective, HUD proposed to require that at least 75 percent of the funds in a city be used principally for the benefit of low- and moderate-income groups. After strong opposition emerged in Congress, HUD altered the proposed regulation in 1978 to say that a city's community development program "shall be presumed" to principally benefit low- and moderate-income persons where not less than 75 percent of the funds was used for the benefit of such persons.[49] For cities whose targeting of funds fell below that percentage figure, HUD provided stricter administrative surveillance to ensure that appropriate emphasis was placed on benefiting lower-income persons. During the Carter administration, federal agencies were more inclined to stress national objectives in administering grants-in-aid than in the Nixon-Ford period, when agencies were told to put authority in regional field offices and to permit subnational governments wide latitude. A Brookings Institution time-series study of the use of Community Development Act funds in sixty-one U.S. cities found that in the first two years of the program (1975–76) officials in only sixteen jurisdictions believed that HUD had a major or determining influence on the content of their community development programs.[50] However, in 1977 officials in almost half of the jurisdictions (twenty-seven cities) thought that HUD's role had expanded, and in 1978 again about half (thirty-one cities) responded the same way.[51]

Urban Policy

Like that of Johnson, Carter's intergovernmental policy stressed the need to assist large cities. Carter announced an urban policy in March 1978 after a year-long study by the Policy Group on Urban and Regional Development. Carter's statement followed a lengthy process of consultation

48. *Housing and Community Development Act of 1977*, Hearings before the Subcommittee on Housing and Community Development of the House Committee on Banking, Finance, and Urban Affairs, 95 Cong. 1 sess. (GPO, 1977), pt. 1, p. 9.
49. 43 Fed. Reg. 8461 (1978). See also Paul R. Dommel and others, *Decentralizing Urban Policy: Case Studies in Community Development* (Brookings Institution, 1982), especially chap. 9.
50. Dommel and others, *Decentralizing Community Development*, p. 69.
51. Dommel and others, *Targeting Community Development*, pp. 38–39.

with groups and organizations in and out of the federal government. Styled a "new partnership to conserve America's communities," the Carter urban policy had no single focal point, but set forth a number of separate goals. As the report of the policy group stated:

The complexity of urban problems makes a meaningful response possible only through a number of different but related policies. No simplistic "centerpiece" policy will achieve our urban commitments. Instead a comprehensive policy approach is necessary.

The broad goals listed in the report for appropriate federal action were to preserve the heritage and values of our older cities; maintain the investment in our older cities and their neighborhoods; assist newer cities in confronting the challenge of growth and pockets of poverty in a fair, efficient and equitable manner; and provide improved housing, job opportunities and community services to the urban poor, minorities and women.[52]

Recommendations to attain these goals included a national development bank to encourage business investment in distressed areas, improved social services in cities, the targeting of federal procurement to urban areas with labor surpluses, additional funds for housing rehabilitation, and a revised general fiscal assistance measure. Carter endorsed the policy group report shortly after he received it.

The Carter program offered relatively little new money for cities. The president's proposals would have increased budget authority by $4.4 billion in fiscal 1979, but the administration estimated that it would increase actual spending by only $742 million in that year. By fiscal 1981 estimated annual spending would be about $2.9 billion. Tax breaks for businesses would amount to approximately $4.9 billion during the first three years of the urban program. Carter's approach focused on improving the use of funds already being directed toward cities and on strengthening the cities' economic infrastructure. It sought to enlist the support of private corporations in the rebuilding of inner cities, treating federal funds as a means to leverage private dollars into cities at a time when federal spending was being contained as much as possible. Carter continued to insist on targeting funds to the most distressed cities and to the most disadvantaged areas within cities. Finally, again reflecting a situation of fiscal constraint, the Carter strategy relied heavily on the coordination, streamlining, and reorientation of grant programs. Despite the elaborate effort at planning, very little resulted from the Carter proposals, largely because of congressional opposition.

52. The President's Urban and Regional Policy Group Report, *A New Partnership to Conserve American Communities* (U.S. Department of Housing and Urban Development, 1978), sec. 3.

ECONOMIC DEVELOPMENT

In the area of employment and economic development, perhaps the most ambitious proposal was for a national development bank to spur private industry to locate in economically depressed areas, especially inner cities. The bank was to provide loan guarantees to enable private financial institutions to finance the capital costs of plant installation, with the goal of reducing interest rates to as little as 2.5 percent. The bank concept encountered a mildly negative reaction in Congress because some members believed that it duplicated the work of the Economic Development Administration (EDA) in the Department of Commerce. To meet this criticism, the president recommended legislation in 1979 that would have brought together elements of his original proposal and the EDA's loan guarantee authority to create a new business development finance program for urban areas. The measure to expand the EDA's powers was passed by both houses in late 1979, but a conference committee was unable to agree on the bill during most of 1980 because of the Senate's opposition to an attempt by House members to add an antirecession public works program to it. By the time that issue was resolved, Republican victories in the November elections had diminished congressional interest in Carter's development plans. Instead, Congress passed at the end of 1980 an extension of existing EDA programs without additional assistance for urban areas.

The other major economic development measure in the Carter urban policy was a labor-intensive public works proposal, offered as a new title XII to the Public Works and Economic Development Act of 1965. The goal of this initiative was to combat structural unemployment by employing people to repair local governments' public facilities. At least 50 percent of all jobs created under the program had to be assigned to the long-term unemployed. Participating communities had to provide 10 percent of the funds, and 10 percent of all program funds nationally had to be spent with minority-owned suppliers and contractors. The Carter administration originally recommended an expenditure of $1 billion annually for three years for this proposal, but dropped it in early 1979 at the time the 1980 budget was submitted.

FISCAL ASSISTANCE PROPOSALS

The president's fiscal assistance legislation centered on a supplemental fiscal assistance bill that initially called for $1.04 billion in fiscal 1979 and $1 billion in fiscal 1980. The measure would have increased the number of communities eligible for assistance under the countercyclical fiscal assistance program from 17,000 to 26,000. When congressional opposition developed, the president in 1979 offered a new measure that combined countercyclical assistance with targeted aid. In the winter of 1979–80 the House and Senate each passed the new Carter proposal, but under different formulas for distributing the aid. Carter withdrew his support for the measure in the spring of 1980 when he announced certain cuts in his 1981 budget recommendations. Both the Senate and House later added their versions of the countercyclical program to bills extending federal revenue sharing, but the countercyclical program was ultimately deleted from the revenue-sharing measure on the House floor. The upshot was that no new fiscal assistance (apart from an extension of revenue sharing) was enacted during the last three Carter years. The original supplementary fiscal assistance program, passed under the Ford administration, had expired in 1978.

COMMUNITY AND HUMAN DEVELOPMENT

Carter made several proposals for community and human development to address the problems of inner cities. One involved a neighborhood self-help development fund designed to provide grants to neighborhood organizations to assist revitalization projects endorsed by local officials. The Carter administration asked for $15 million for the program. Congress enacted the measure for fiscal 1979 and fiscal 1980 at the level requested, but reduced the funding to $10 million for fiscal 1981. Congress also authorized assistance to localities for developing recreation services and cultural programs in poor neighborhoods, but funded it in 1979 and 1980 at levels below the administration's requests. In the 1981 budget Congress denied further funding to both programs.

ADMINISTRATIVE COORDINATION

Carter's legislative initiatives were so unsuccessful that administrative action assumed considerable importance in the effort to create an urban program. In August 1978 the president issued four executive orders to effect a more focused attack on the problems of distressed cities. These orders directed the General Services Administration, administrator of the federal government's office facilities, to consider the impact of site and space selection on cities' central business districts and employment opportunities; required federal agencies to emphasize procurement in labor surplus areas; established an interagency coordinating council to cooperate on urban policy measures; and required the Office of Management and

Budget to develop criteria for agencies to use in analyzing the impact of major policy initiatives on urban areas. Carter also continued the efforts of preceding administrations to improve the management of categorical grants by standardizing planning, application, reporting, and accounting requirements.[53] However, Carter generally opposed the Nixon policy of administrative decentralization in federal departments. Under Carter regional office staffs diminished, and authority over federal grant programs tended to return to Washington.

Slowing Functional Growth and Changing Allocations

During the Johnson and Nixon-Ford administrations, the annual growth in federal aid to states and localities was usually greater than increases in other parts of the federal budget. Under Johnson, for instance, the rate of yearly increase approached 25 percent. At the outset of the Carter administration, it appeared that the spending rise would continue, but this situation soon changed.

Between the announcement of the Carter urban policy in March 1978 and the submission of the 1980 federal budget in early 1979, California voters adopted Proposition 13, which substantially reduced local real estate taxes and received a large amount of national publicity. Constitutional limitations on government spending began to be discussed in a number of state legislatures as well as in Congress. A gradually increasing rate of inflation made the situation more serious; in 1978, the rate was 7.7 percent, up from 6.5 percent in 1977. A mood of fiscal caution, if not rebellion, spread across the country, affecting the behavior of governments. Carter seemed to respond in his 1980 budget recommendations, which asked for funding for only a few of his urban initiatives. The increase requested for grants-in-aid in the 1980 budget was only 1 percent over the figure estimated for fiscal 1979. Much the same sense of fiscal restraint dominated the preparation of the 1981 budget. In January 1980 Carter asked for a spending total of $96.3 billion in grants-in-aid, but that figure was reduced by about $5 billion in March when the president requested an overall reduction of about $15 billion in the proposed 1981 budget.[54]

Table 7 shows that funding for federal grants grew by about $26 billion during the Carter presidency, or slightly less than 10 percent per year, a

53. Rochelle Stanfield, "What Has 500 Parts, Costs $83 Billion, and Is Condemned by Almost Everybody?" *National Journal*, vol. 13 (January 3, 1981), p. 7.

54. *Fiscal Year 1981 Budget Revisions*, pt. 1 (GPO, 1980).

Table 7. *Functional Changes in Federal Aid Outlays, Fiscal Years
1977 and 1981*

Function	1977 Amount (millions of dollars)	1977 Percentage of total	1981 Amount (millions of dollars)	1981 Percentage of total
Defense and veterans	175	0.3	149	0.2
Agriculture	371	0.5	829	0.9
Natural resources and environment	4,188	6.1	4,944	5.2
Commerce and transportation	8,317	12.2	13,466	14.2
Community and regional development	4,496	6.6	6,124	6.5
Education, health, welfare, manpower (excluding public assistance)	34,119	49.9	52,920	55.8
Public assistance	6,351	9.3	8,462	8.9
Energy	74	0.1	617	0.7
Law enforcement	713	1.0	333	0.4
General government aid	9,592	14.0	6,918	7.3
Total	68,396	100.0	94,762	100.0

Source: *Special Analyses, Fiscal Years 1979, 1983.* Figures are rounded.

rate of increase that did not quite match the rate of inflation. By the middle
of Carter's term of office, federal aid's proportion of the budgets of subnational governments had begun to drop.

In January 1980 the Carter administration recommended a continuation
of the federal revenue-sharing program, which was to expire September
30, 1980, but in April, to counteract strong inflationary pressures, the
president modified his proposal to exclude the state governments. To assist
localities that had been receiving a portion of the states' share of federal
revenue sharing, the administration proposed a $500 million transitional
fund for 1981 and 1982. Congress concurred in the decision to drop the
states, but after considerable debate rejected the transitional fund idea.
Accepting another Carter recommendation, Congress all but deleted the
law enforcement and assistance programs that had begun during the Johnson administration. In the 1981 budget, Congress reduced funding for the
Law Enforcement Assistance Administration to slightly more than $100
million (down from nearly $500 million in 1980), and most of these remaining
funds were earmarked for one grant program only—the Juvenile Justice
and Delinquency Prevention Act of 1974.

Programs that grew most rapidly in dollar amounts during the Carter years were in the areas of social welfare and transportation; increases in these two categories accounted for about 90 percent of the $26 billion growth in federal aid. Medicaid continued under Carter, as it had under the Republicans, to show the largest dollar increase of any assistance program. Grants rose from $9.9 billion in 1977 to $16.8 billion in 1981. Nutrition and housing assistance also expanded significantly between 1977 and 1981: nutrition grants grew from $3.4 billion to $5.2 billion and housing assistance payments rose from $1.8 billion to $4.0 billion. In 1977 Congress added a new program, energy assistance grants for low-income households. It authorized $1.6 billion in emergency aid during the winter of 1979–80 and approximately $3 billion in fiscal 1981. Spending under the ESEA, which was reauthorized for five years in 1978, increased by about $1 billion during Carter's term. Title I of the ESEA (compensatory education grants) was modified to provide additional funds to school districts most severely afflicted by poverty. Employment and training assistance grants were about $1.5 billion greater in 1981 than in 1977, although they had declined from their 1978 level. By the end of Carter's administration the CETA program was being curtailed.

Federal grants for transportation facilities increased significantly under this administration. In November 1978 Carter signed legislation providing approximately $54 billion in aid for highways and mass transit facilities over a four-year period. The measure emphasized the restoration and maintenance of existing highways and was less concerned with new construction than earlier legislation. Although the president approved the legislation, total funding was about $7 billion higher than he had requested. Congress rejected an administration proposal to decrease the federal share of most transportation programs.

The changing budget allocations in the Carter years caused the grant system to differ in certain respects from the pattern in the Republican period. The proportion of funds for general-purpose assistance and block grants, which was 26.1 percent of all grants in 1977 (see table 4), dropped to 17.8 percent in 1981. Budget cuts under Carter affected broad-based programs most deeply. Transfer programs, such as medicaid and nutrition and housing assistance, which were less susceptible to budget cutbacks, grew in relation to other types of grants. In 1977 these programs, taken together, constituted 34.9 percent of federal aid dollars. By 1981, their proportion had risen to 42.1 percent.

Reagan's First Two Years, 1981–83

In 1980 the economic problems that afflicted the Carter administration were getting worse. The rate of inflation, which was about 6 percent when the president took office, had grown to over 13 percent. The rate of unemployment had also begun to rise, moving from under 6 percent in 1979 to slightly over 7 percent. Republican presidential candidate Ronald Reagan, an ideological conservative, blamed the Democrats and a government that under them, he said, had grown too big. Reagan told the Republican convention in his acceptance speech:

I believe it is clear our federal government is overgrown and overweight. . . . I will not accept the excuse that the federal government has grown so big and powerful that it is beyond the control of any president, any administration, or Congress. We are going to put an end to the notion that the American taxpayer exists to fund the federal government.[55]

As one way to slow the federal government's growth, Reagan suggested returning some programs to states and localities. While he echoed the complaints of Richard Nixon that the federal government intervened too much in local affairs, his solution was more drastic than redesigning grants-in-aid to give the recipients more freedom. He promised:

Everything that can be run more effectively by state and local government we shall turn over to state and local government, along with the funding sources to pay for it. We are going to put an end to the money merry-go-round where our money becomes Washington's money, to be spent by the states and cities exactly the way the federal bureaucrats tell them to.[56]

Functional Area Reductions

The most significant impact the Reagan administration made on the grant system in its first two years in office was in the level of federal assistance expenditures. In February 1981 Reagan proposed more than $40 billion in reductions in the 1982 budget submitted by outgoing President Carter. He also called for a tax cut in 1982 of $53.9 billion, beginning with a 10 percent reduction in individual income taxes in July 1981, and additional 10 percent cuts in each of the next two years. Reagan's budget

55. *Congressional Quarterly Almanac*, vol. 36 (1980), p. 37B.
56. Ibid.

cuts slowed the rate of growth for most domestic programs, eliminated a few, and consolidated a substantial number of categorical grants into block grants. The president's general objective was to lower by about half (from 12 percent to 7 percent) the annual rate of federal budget increases in the 1982–86 period, compared to the 1976–81 period.[57] Because he wished to increase defense spending and to maintain at current levels most income transfer ("safety net") programs, the burden of his reduction fell on programs outside these areas, including many grants to state and local governments.

The Ninety-seventh Congress, composed of a Republican-controlled Senate and a Democratic House of Representatives in which conservative Democrats and Republicans had a working majority, enacted most of the president's recommendations in the first eight months of the 1981 session.[58]

As table 8 shows, federal assistance after Reagan's first two years dropped about $1.75 billion below the funding level that existed when Carter left office. When inflation is considered, the significance of the reduction is greater. Between 1981 and 1983 federal grants to states and localities decreased from 19.5 percent of federal domestic outlays to 16.1 percent and from 25.1 percent of state and local expenditures to 21.8 percent. In fiscal 1983 grants to subnational governments accounted for the lowest percentage of the federal domestic budget since the early 1960s, before the Great Society initiatives. They made up the smallest proportion of state and local expenditures since 1971, before the advent of revenue sharing, CETA, and the community development block grant program.

Funding levels were reduced in a variety of programs. In 1982 Congress passed a new block grant program, the Job Training Partnership Act (JTPA), to replace CETA. Under the JTPA, private-sector employment was emphasized and, unlike CETA, no funds were provided for public service jobs. Grants for employment and training assistance declined from about $6 billion in 1981 to slightly over $3 billion in 1983. Assistance to states and localities for the construction of wastewater treatment plants decreased by nearly $1 billion in the 1981–83 period, from $3.9 billion to $3.0 billion. In 1981 Congress approved a measure to reduce the federal financial share

57. "Reagan's Budget Cuts: The Reasons Why," *National Journal*, vol. 13 (February 21, 1981), p. 305.

58. For a discussion of grant reductions in 1981, see John William Ellwood, ed., *Reductions in U.S. Domestic Spending* (Transaction Books, 1982), chap. 4. The impact of the reductions is examined in Richard P. Nathan, Fred C. Doolittle, and associates, *The Consequences of Cuts: The Effects of the Reagan Domestic Program on State and Local Governments* (Princeton Urban and Regional Research Center, 1983).

Table 8. *Functional Changes in Federal Aid Outlays, Fiscal Years 1981 and 1983*

	1981		1983	
Function	Amount (millions of dollars)	Percentage of total	Amount (millions of dollars)	Percentage of total
Defense and veterans	149	0.2	152	0.2
Agriculture	829	0.9	1,822	2.0
Natural resources and environment	4,944	5.2	4,018	4.3
Commerce and transportation	13,466	14.2	13,310	14.3
Community and regional development	6,124	6.5	4,962	5.3
Education, health, welfare, manpower (excluding public assistance)	52,920	55.8	53,781	58.0
Public assistance	8,462	8.9	7,844	8.4
Energy	617	0.7	482	0.5
Law enforcement	333	0.4	101	0.1
General government aid	6,918	7.3	6,541	7.0
Total	94,762	100.0	93,013	100.0

Source: *Special Analyses, Fiscal Years 1983, 1985*. Figures are rounded.

of treatment plant construction from 75 percent (set in the 1972 Federal Water Pollution Control Act Amendments) to 55 percent, beginning in fiscal 1985. It also limited the types of construction eligible for federal support. Another area in which grants diminished was urban mass transit assistance. Congress rejected a Reagan administration proposal submitted in 1981 to terminate grants used for operating subsidies of transit systems by 1985, but it did lower the overall funding. Grant outlays for transit assistance decreased from $3.8 billion in 1981 to $3.6 billion in 1983. Grants administered by the Department of Commerce for economic development assistance programs declined by almost 40 percent during 1981–83. Smaller proportionate reductions were made in grants under title I of the ESEA and in the community development block grant program.

Some programs survived relatively well despite the general cutbacks, including the social services block grant and most health grants. The medicaid program grew, but at a somewhat slower rate than in the Carter years. Federal medicaid grants increased from $16.8 billion to $19.0 billion. Congress rejected an administration proposal to place a fixed ceiling on federal medicaid expenditures, but it did vote to reduce the amount each state would otherwise be entitled to receive by 3 percent in fiscal 1982, 4 percent in fiscal 1983, and 4.5 percent in fiscal 1985. In 1982 it allowed states to require medicaid beneficiaries to pay certain fees for medical services. Nutrition grants grew from $5.2 billion in 1981 to $6.4 billion in 1983; housing assistance payments increased from $4.0 to $5.7 billion. While other grants declined by approximately $6.6 billion in the first two years under Reagan, transfer programs rose about $4.9 billion and in 1983 composed nearly half (48.2 percent) of the federal aid package. Estimates in the fiscal 1984 and fiscal 1985 budgets indicated that transfer programs' proportion of grant dollars would remain at about that level.

Changes in the Design of Grants

While program reductions constituted the most important part of the Reagan administration's grant policy in its first two years, changes also took place in the design of grants. Early in 1981 the president proposed a series of block grants to consolidate approximately eighty categorical programs. Unlike the block grants of the Nixon years, when higher levels of funding accompanied the new forms of subvention, block grants were perceived by the Reagan administration as a way of reducing outlays. In creating seven new block grants in 1981, mainly in the fields of health and education, Congress reduced the funding of the consolidated programs from 10 to 35 percent. Moreover, the president professed to regard block grants merely as a transition to more extreme forms of devolution. He told the National Conference of State Legislatures in mid-1981:

The ultimate objective . . . is to use block grants . . . only as a bridge, leading to the day when you'll have not only the responsibility for the programs that properly belong at the State level, but you will have the tax sources now usurped by Washington returned to you, ending that roundtrip of the people's money to Washington, where a carrying charge is deducted, and then back to you.[59]

The new block grants all were directed to the states, and in a number of cases programs that had provided funds directly to localities were redesigned to increase the role of the state governments. As an example, the program of discretionary grants to small cities within the community development block grants, which had been operated as a federal-local program, was revised to authorize states to develop their own programs of community development grants for local governments. In the JTPA

59. *Public Papers: Reagan, 1981* (GPO, 1982), p. 682.

block grant program, the governor's office was given much greater authority than it had had under CETA. Under the JTPA the governor was largely responsible for the designation of the service delivery areas within which the program operated. In other block grants, the states replaced such local units as county governments, school districts, and local health organizations as funding recipients, although pass-through provisions were incorporated in several cases.

Reagan's New Federalism

In his 1982 State of the Union address, the president proposed his own "new federalism" consisting of a "swap" and "turnback" to sort out functions in the federal system. This was necessary, he said, because "a maze of interlocking jurisdictions and levels of government confronts average citizens in trying to solve even the simplest of problems. They don't know where to turn for answers, who to hold accountable, who to praise, who to blame, who to vote for or against."[60]

Under the swap, the federal government was to take full responsibility for the medicaid program and the states were to assume authority for the AFDC and food stamp programs.[61] (Later in the year, food stamps were dropped from the proposed swap.) The turnback involved the eventual reassignment to the states by 1988 of sixty-one federal grant programs, including the 1981 block grants and seven block grants newly proposed by the president. These programs constituted approximately one-third of all grant funds in Reagan's 1983 budget. To assist the states in financing the reassigned programs, a trust fund, supported from federal excise taxes, was to be established during 1984–87. During this period states could use their share of the trust fund to employ federal agencies to operate the programs, but they could also use the money for other purposes. During 1988–91 the trust fund was to be phased out, and states would be allowed to pick up specific excise taxes that the federal government would promise to forgo, with which the states could maintain the programs or support other activities. After 1984 the affected programs would not operate as grants-in-aid, with federal appropriations managed by federal agencies.

State and local officials sharply questioned the administration's claim that their jurisdictions would gain financially from the swap and turnback.

60. *Public Papers: Reagan, 1982*, p. 75
61. For an analysis, see *National Journal*, vol. 14 (February 27, 1982).

Despite intense efforts, Reagan officials were unable to work out compromises with these officials. In the absence of their support, the administration failed to propose even draft legislation in the second session of the Ninety-seventh Congress. In 1983 the administration did submit a revised "new federalism" proposal to Congress, but the congressional response was limited to hearings conducted by the Joint Economic Committee in March. Prospects for dramatic change in devolution policies appear dim at best.

Conclusion

In the volume of federal dollars expended, the grant-in-aid system virtually doubled in the four Johnson years, and then almost quadrupled in the following eight years under Nixon and Ford. It began to grow at a slower rate in the Carter administration. Under the Great Society, the federal government began for the first time to provide assistance to subnational governments in most areas of domestic policy. That support continued and expanded under Nixon's New Federalism, although administration interest at that time centered on giving more latitude to local officials in using federal dollars. By the mid-1970s federal assistance to subnational governments was so extensive that issues of grant design became crucial. The "new partnership" of Jimmy Carter was largely an effort to target existing grant programs to the benefit of distressed urban areas.

Some variation in grant-in-aid policies was attributable to the policies of the party of each president. Democrats Lyndon Johnson and Jimmy Carter tried to develop explicit urban policies through which federal aid would be directed toward the problems of metropolitan areas. Republicans Richard Nixon and Gerald Ford were less inclined to highlight urban areas as such, even though their programs did result in much increased aid to local governments. In Republican years federal assistance tended to spread among all general-purpose local governments, whether urban, suburban, or rural. Another difference was that Republican administrations favored providing recipient jurisdictions with more latitude in the use of grant dollars. Under Democratic presidents the pursuit of national goals was stressed, and surveillance over subnational governments grew.

However, other significant developments during the four administrations had little or nothing to do with party differences. Johnson and Nixon tended to discuss federal system issues in broad, ideological terms, whereas

Ford and Carter focused more on technical matters. As grant-in-aid expenditures grew, presidents became more concerned with managing and controlling programs. National economic performance began to dictate the direction of grant policies more than party platforms could. Another aspect of grant-in-aid policy where no party difference seemed detectable concerned the choice of whether to assist states as opposed to local governments. The Johnson and Carter administrations clearly favored cities as recipients, a view consistent with their emphasis on the pursuit of explicit urban policies. The Republicans generally gave greater attention to the role of the states in their party platforms and campaigns, but they also presided over large increases in aid to local governments. They needed the support of a Democratic Congress for enactment of revenue sharing and other broad-based grants, and the designation of local governments as recipients increased the appeal of their innovative grant designs.

To help understand the impact of the Reagan administration, it is useful to consider how its policies differ from those of the four preceding administrations. Certainly Reagan is not the first president to cut the federal budget. Carter sought to reduce his 1981 budget by approximately $15 billion in March 1980 from its January level because of accelerating inflation. Further, the budget cuts both Carter and Reagan made were foreshadowed by a slowdown in the late 1970s in state and local spending. Between 1975 and 1981 state and local spending as a share of GNP declined from 15 percent to 13 percent.[62] Some of the programs that Reagan curtailed are ones that Carter also sought to reduce; an example is CETA. Arguably, too, Reagan's attempt to use block grants represents a continuity. Block grants were unknown in grant policy until the Johnson administration, but emerged as a significant category of federal aid in the Nixon and Ford administrations.

On the other hand, Reagan's attitude toward grants-in-aid differs in at least two major respects from the policies followed by all four of his predecessors. Federal budget reductions under Reagan have disproportionately focused on grants to states and localities, whereas in all four of the preceding administrations grants for subnational governments grew in both dollar amounts and (except in the last half of Carter's term) as a share of the federal budget. The president's fiscal 1985 budget estimated that as a proportion of federal domestic outlays grants would decrease to 15.4

62. George E. Peterson, "The State and Local Sector," in John Palmer and Isabel Sawhill, eds., *The Reagan Experiment* (Urban Institute, 1982), p. 160.

percent by 1987. The decline in grants may be attributable partly to the fact that many of them, particularly grants to expand the services of subnational governments (as distinct from ones providing payments to individuals), are "controllable." That is, as budget items they are subject to discretionary reductions by the president and Congress without changes in existing law, and thus are exceptionally vulnerable to a president determined to cut federal spending. Yet the Reagan administration's reductions appear to reflect a philosophy of federalism as well. Reagan seems to want a return to the principle of dual federalism, in which the federal government and the states each would have their own separate responsibilities.

The Reagan administration is distinctive, too, for its clear preference for working with state governments. This position is consistent in principle with a strict sorting out of constitutional functions, inasmuch as the cities, as mere legal subdivisions of the states, are not constitutionally an independent level of government. Both Democratic and Republican presidents during 1965–80 tended to bypass the states and develop direct federal-city relations, whereas the Reagan administration prefers to funnel federal aid to localities through the states, in keeping with constitutional tradition.

Presidential preferences in grant policies depend on congressional approval, and thus far the Congress has been much more willing to endorse Reagan's reductions in grant spending than his structural revisions in intergovernmental relations. Thus, even though states and localities will undoubtedly have to assume more of the fiscal burden of operating their governments, a return to the grant-in-aid pattern of the pre-1965 years, when federal assistance applied to only a handful of programs, seems unlikely.

LAWRENCE D. BROWN

The Politics of Devolution in Nixon's New Federalism

IN THE 1960s federal programs of grants-in-aid to state and local governments "exploded" (to use an alarmist term much favored by the system's
critics), and certain peculiar features of the politics of American federalism
came in for increasingly severe criticism. In particular, the tendency of
the central government to pile one special-purpose program upon another[1]
and the unwillingness of that government to consolidate and simplify the
system extensively have led some to accuse it of political and administrative
irrationality. Questions about the proper degree of federal specificity and
control in the design of programs to be carried out by states and localities
are not new, of course; they go back to the founding of the nation, received
thoughtful attention after the "rise of a new federalism" in the New Deal,[2]
and were discussed intermittently in the 1950s. By the late 1960s, however,
federally engendered "overload" (to use another staple term of what Richard

Timothy Conlon and Martha Derthick offered helpful comments on earlier versions of
this chapter. Special thanks are due to Richard P. Nathan, Robert F. Cook, and several of
their associates in the Princeton Urban and Regional Research Center, who made many
useful suggestions at a seminar on the chapter. The author thanks William F. Burgess for
research assistance and David E. Morse and Joan P. Milan for typing assistance.

1. By one count the number of grant programs increased from 160 in 1962 to 1,030 by
1976: cited in Samuel H. Beer, "Federalism, Nationalism, and Democracy in America,"
American Political Science Review, vol. 72 (March 1978), p. 18. The exclusion of unfunded
authorizations, however, yields 442 (for fiscal year 1975). Advisory Commission on Intergovernmental Relations, *A Catalog of Federal Grant-in-Aid Programs to State and Local
Government: Grants Funded FY 1975*, A-52a (ACIR, October 1977), p. 1.

2. The phrase is taken from Jane Perry Clark, *The Rise of a New Federalism: Federal-
State Cooperation in the United States* (Columbia University Press, 1938). Another New
Deal–era study is V. O. Key, Jr., *The Administration of Federal Grants to States* (Chicago:
Public Administration Service for the Committee on Public Administration of the Social
Science Research Council, 1937).

Nathan has called the "henny-penny" school of federalism)[3] was widely believed to have reached "crisis" proportions. Critics charged that federal grant programs were both too numerous and too narrowly drawn; that these programs sapped the political discretion and "vitality" of state and local governments by foreclosing choice at these levels; and that the programs were both inefficient and ineffective because they required state and local governments to honor uniform federal priorities, not divergent local needs.

Proposed alternatives take many forms, three of which are of special importance. These are: an accepted division of functions between the central and the subnational governments that would preserve a large area of independence for the latter (sorting out); an agreement by the central government to give a certain percentage of its annual tax receipts or an annual appropriation to state or local governments for unrestricted purposes (revenue sharing); and consolidation of several categorical grants into a larger, more flexible package to be used for broader, but nonetheless delimited, purposes (block grants).

These alternatives, which may be captured by the general phrase "devolution strategies," have been discussed intermittently throughout American history. (Reichley credits Henry Clay with the first revenue-sharing proposal in the 1820s.)[4] In the 1940s and 1950s various scholars in the field of public administration endorsed block grants as an essentially managerial device for overcoming fragmentation and improving coordination in federal programs involving the states and localities. The first Hoover Commission supported this view, and the Truman administration recommended block grants for some public health and welfare programs. These proposals failed to pass Congress.[5] In 1953 the Eisenhower administration empaneled the Kestnbaum Commission to make a study of federal programs that might be turned over to the states,[6] and in 1958 Congressman Melvin Laird,

3. Richard P. Nathan, " 'Reforming' the Federal Grant-in-Aid System for States and Localities," National Tax Association, May 18, 1981, pp. 8–10.
4. A. James Reichley, Conservatives in an Age of Change: The Nixon and Ford Administrations (Brookings Institution, 1981), p. 154.
5. See Timothy J. Conlon, "Congressional Response to the New Federalism: The Block Grant Experience" (Ph.D. dissertation, Harvard University, 1982), chap. 2, for an excellent review of early efforts.
6. On the (Kestnbaum) Commission on Intergovernmental Relations, see W. Brooke Graves, American Intergovernmental Relations (Scribner's, 1964), pp. 892–900. On its successor, the Joint Federal-State Action Committee (1957–59), see ibid., pp. 461–63, 900–03; and Morton Grodzins, The American System (Rand McNally, 1966), pp. 308–16.

Republican of Wisconsin, introduced the first "modern" revenue-sharing bill.[7] Nothing happened. In the 1960s the pace of grant-in-aid expansion quickened along with economic growth, and liberal Democrats grew interested in revenue sharing as a means of allocating the federal "fiscal dividend" that would ensue as revenues exceeded expenditures.[8] Between 1964 and 1968 the pace of grant expansion became very fast indeed. Complaints were voiced about fragmentation, balkanization, rigidity, red tape, and more.[9] The earlier emphasis on consolidation began to give way to an explicit concern for decentralization as well: block grants might not only improve administrative management and program coordination, but might also protect the vitality of state and local governments against an increasingly dominant federal government. Still, little happened.[10] A few programs—model cities, the partnership for health, and the Law Enforcement Assistance Administration (LEAA), for example—were essentially block grants, giving states, localities, or both wide discretion in the use of funds, but the number of new categoricals continued to grow, and it came to be widely accepted that far-reaching devolution was politically infeasible.[11]

The situation then changed suddenly and dramatically as proposals put forth by the Nixon administration were passed. In 1972 Congress passed the State and Local Fiscal Assistance Act, creating general revenue sharing. In 1973 it enacted the Comprehensive Employment and Training Act (CETA), folding seventeen manpower programs into one broader package. In 1974 it adopted the community development block grant program (CDBG) in the Housing and Community Development Act, combining several categorical programs into a single more flexible grant. Whereas 98 percent of federal aid had been in categorical grants in 1966, the percentage

7. H.R. 12080 was "a bill to provide financial assistance to the states by returning to the states a portion of the Federal income taxes collected therein." *Congressional Record* (April 22, 1958), p. 6953.

8. On the Heller-Pechman plan, see Richard P. Nathan and Susannah E. Calkins, "The Story of Revenue Sharing," in Robert L. Peabody, ed., *Cases in American Politics* (Praeger, 1976), pp. 11–43, especially pp. 15–19.

9. For example, *Creative Federalism*, Hearings before the Subcommittee on Intergovernmental Relations of the Senate Committee on Government Operations, 90 Cong. 1 sess. (Government Printing Office, 1967), especially pts. 2-A and 2-B. See also the overview in Deil S. Wright, *Federal Grants-in-Aid: Perspectives and Alternatives* (American Enterprise Institute for Public Policy Research, 1968).

10. Nathan and Calkins, "The Story of Revenue Sharing," pp. 15–20.

11. For instance, Edward C. Banfield, "Revenue Sharing in Theory and Practice," *The Public Interest*, no. 23 (Spring 1971), pp. 33–45.

had fallen to 75 by 1975.[12] The system had not been transformed, but it had been modified quite beyond expectation.

The obvious question is, why? What new political configurations produced changes long dismissed as incompatible with American politics as usual? A less obvious, but equally important, question is, why not more? The Nixon administration had called not only for the three programs enacted, but also for block grants (or "special" revenue sharing) for law enforcement, education, rural development, and transportation programs—none of which was adopted. Was grant "reform" an overdue response to long-felt needs and a harbinger of new political support for a more rational federalism? Or was it a more or less accidental and limited political event that signals no deviation from the fragmentary tendencies of the past? And whichever may be the case, why is it so?

The individual success stories—general revenue sharing, CETA, and CDBG—have received some sophisticated attention from political scientists.[13] These studies, however, have not pursued a fascinating comparative question: how did it happen that of the original Nixon proposals (general revenue sharing and six special revenue-sharing packages), three managed to pass, but not the others? Are there common political properties among the successes that are lacking in the case of the four "failures"?[14]

Some may contend that the explanation is straightforward: the essence of devolution as enacted in the early 1970s was an orgy of distributive politics, what Beer calls "promiscuous localism."[15] The categoricals confined aid to jurisdictions that met statutory, administrative, or improvised criteria of need and capacity, and thus ran against the grain of "parochial

12. Beer, "Federalism, Nationalism, and Democracy," p. 18.

13. Major works on which this chapter relies heavily are: Paul R. Dommel, *The Politics of Revenue Sharing* (Indiana University Press, 1974); Samuel H. Beer, "The Adoption of General Revenue Sharing: A Case Study in Public Sector Politics," *Public Policy*, vol. 24 (Spring 1976), pp. 127–95: Nathan and Calkins, "The Story of Revenue Sharing"; Roger H. Davidson, *The Politics of Comprehensive Manpower Legislation* (John Hopkins University Press, 1972); Richard L. Cole, "The Politics of Housing and Community Development in America: The Housing and Community Development Act of 1974," in David A. Caputo, ed., *The Politics of Policy Making in America: Five Case Studies* (W. H. Freeman, 1977), pp. 100–31; and Gary Orfield, *Congressional Power: Congress and Social Change* (Harcourt Brace Jovanovich, 1975), pp. 165–71. Also useful is Michael D. Reagan and John G. Sanzone, *The New Federalism*, 2d ed. (Oxford University Press, 1981), especially chaps. 4 and 5.

14. For a stimulating (and as yet unpublished) treatment of such questions, see Conlon, "Congressional Response to the New Federalism"; and Timothy J. Conlon, "Back in Vogue: The Politics of Block Grant Legislation," *Intergovernmental Perspective*, vol. 7 (Spring 1981), pp. 8–15.

15. Beer, "The Adoption of General Revenue Sharing," p. 148.

and particularistic" legislative politics in the Congress. The general revenue-sharing formula gave new unrestricted federal aid to virtually every
government jurisdiction in the country, and the CETA and CDBG programs greatly expanded the ranks of jurisdictions receiving manpower and
development money. In this view the irresistible distributive logic of
diffusion, carried along by logrolling and bargaining, is a sufficient explanation.

That distributive politics had a hand in the outcome is undeniable; that
they are the basis of an adequate explanation is doubtful. The "realist"
argument faces two problems. First, indulgent distributive politics do not
(at least not on their face) explain the *scope* of the outcome, that is, why
some devolution proposals passed while others failed. Second, they fail to
explain the *timing* of the outcome. Parochial and particularistic Congress
may be, but the facts are: (1) for years it strongly supported categorical
programs whose allocation was heavily influenced, if not determined, by
bureaucratic discretion; (2) it showed indifference or hostility to devolution
proposals; (3) the pressure for devolution came from the executive, not
from Congress; and (4) the legislature agreed to enact three proposals only
after long debate, many reservations, and extensive modifications. These
considerations do not invalidate the distributive explanation, but they do
suggest that it is but one element in a more complex constellation of
variables.

It is the argument of this essay that the scope and timing of the devolution
successes are best explained by three variables, here briefly named "values," "structure," and "strategy." In the three success cases, the three
variables had experienced changes and then interacted politically in ways
favorable to enactment, whereas in the four failure cases they had not and
did not.

In the pages to follow, the term *values* means normative views on the
desirable and proper workings of government. These views include both
general and contextual positions (for example, the proper role of the federal
government in protecting minority rights and interests) and evaluations of
specific governmental efforts (for instance, whether manpower programs
are "well" run). *Structure* means more or less stable relationships within
and among institutions. It includes both public power structures (for
example, relations between president and Congress, between congressional subcommittees, or among levels of government in the federal system)
and private ones (for instance, internal politics within and among unions,
professional associations, business groups, or other special interests that

seek to influence public policy). *Strategy* means those discrete elements of policy that politicians may manipulate (such as the terms of a formula) in hopes of building or preventing a coalition to win initiation of a proposal in the executive branch or enactment in Congress. The rough model employed here is that legislation begins life in the general values and specific evaluative perceptions held by a wide range of political actors, makes its way into the public and private power structures that may promote or block it, and is then transformed by negotiating strategies that do or do not generate a coalition for enactment.

The Normative Context

Arguments about the merits of *policy devolution* are not self-contained; they are inseparable from perceptions and evaluations of the meaning of *political decentralization.* Constitutional design and continuities in political culture have made the American political system extremely decentralized: the power of the public sector is limited by arrangements that share collective decisonmaking with the private sector (privatism), divide power among three levels of government (federalism), and separate power among major institutions at each of these levels (separation of powers). The founding fathers were at pains to explain the advantages of such a system: it would reduce the risks of tyranny, contain the dangers of both factions and mass movements, and secure the benefits of representative government. Some proponents of devolution have viewed their preferred strategy as an obvious and logical implication of these arrangements. Advocates of revenue sharing and block grants have frequently invoked hoary passages from Jefferson, de Tocqueville, and others as evidence that a larger role for state and local governments in running federal programs will prevent a dangerous concentration of power at the center, bring government "closer to the people," and give citizens a training ground in democratic practices.[16] Others, however, have sharply questioned this logic. They have pointed out that political decentralization is compatible with various approaches to fiscal federalism and is in itself neutral among them. They have argued

16. For example, Alexis de Tocqueville, *Democracy in America*, vol. 1 (Knopf, 1945), pp. 42, 63, 69–71, 94–96, 99–100, 260–61; and Thomas Jefferson, "On Citizenship," in Mary L. Pollingue, ed., *Readings in American Government*, 2d ed. (Dubuque, Iowa: Kendall/ Hunt, 1978), pp. 69–70. For an overview, see Anwar Syed, *The Political Theory of American Local Government* (Random House, 1966).

too that policy devolution may impose important costs and risks in a highly decentralized political system.

Several deeply rooted elements of the American value system generate opposition to extensive policy devolution. Revenue sharing, block grants, and the like are not merely distributional techniques for the achievement of agreed-upon ends; their perceived merits are inseparable from broader attitudes toward the role of the central government in the U.S. federal system. Throughout much of its history, the United States followed a policy of modified laissez-faire, extending governmental deference to the private sector whenever feasible. When public action became necessary, American doctrine preferred that state and local, not the central, government be the port of first call. Thus central governmental action generally was a course of third resort, so to speak, the main exceptions being collective goods (an army, the currency), advancement of infant industries, and internal improvements.

Aid to individuals went mainly to the "deserving" poor, those who were unable through no fault of their own to capitalize on the equality of opportunity extended by the American economy. Such welfare was first a private and then mainly a state and local responsibility. When exceptions were made—for example, on a large scale in the New Deal—they did not spring directly from a broad mandate for redistribution among social classes or from the agenda of disaffected groups. Rather, they mainly drew upon the analytical and advocacy efforts of middle- and upper-class reformers who had put their reforms on the public agenda by means of a series of commissions and organizational activities, then watched the federal government flail about in search of means of coping with the Depression, and worked to persuade New Deal policymakers of the merits of their ideas and to build political coalitions for their enactment.[17] From these ad hoc coalitions came social security, unemployment compensation, aid to the blind and disabled, and aid to families with dependent children.

Various categories of need came to be recognized, documented, legitimized, and addressed over time. In most cases, however, the recognition of need as universal—that is, dependent on objective attributes of the client and logically independent of place—was balanced by recognition of the value of local diversity and discretion. With the principal exception of social security, fully federal programs were not acceptable. In most cases

17. See, for example, Arthur M. Schlesinger, Jr., *The Age of Roosevelt: The Coming of the New Deal* (Houghton Mifflin, 1959), chaps. 16, 18.

the federal government split both funding and responsibility with state or local governments. The federal grants-in-aid were quid pro quos—money extended to state and local governments to induce them to do things they would otherwise decline to do, delay, or underfund, and to do them in ways (with professional skill, responsible administration, and fiscal rectitude) federal policymakers thought desirable.[18] The system allowed the states and localities to run the programs, but the federal government could impose substantive and administrative constraints. The system allowed liberals to *bring* federal aid to the truly needy, while conservatives *confined* aid to the truly needy. The categorical grant-in-aid system was in essence a political and ideological compromise, and the rigidities of the system were inherent to its political character.

These processes of recognition, documentation, debate, legitimation, and categorization continued slowly in the Truman, Eisenhower, and Kennedy years, but in 1964 new political conditions (Johnson's landslide victory, the election of sixty-seven new liberal Democrats to the House, and a national sense that a clogged agenda was waiting to be unblocked) led to many new programs.[19] For the most part, however, these programs were fully consistent with the political values of the past: program design faithfully reflected the perceived nature and limits of need and merit. Federal aid to pay the hospital bills of the elderly was judged worthy; aid for the medical bills of the whole population (national health insurance) was not. Medical assistance for welfare families was acceptable; for the nonpoor, not. People suffering from inadequate nutrition came to be recognized as deserving, and the food stamp program was expanded to deal with their problem. It was agreed that decent housing was not available to all Americans, and new subsidy programs were added to earlier, feeble public housing efforts. In-kind programs addressing limited categories of recognized need and merit were politically acceptable; general cash aid allocated on the criterion of poverty alone was not. Indeed, some policymakers held the utopian view that poverty, like certain forms of disease, was a condition preventable by timely public intervention to develop "human capital." Poverty was viewed as an unfortunate cycle, in which

18. Phillip Monypenny, "Federal Grants-in-Aid to State Governments: A Political Analysis," *National Tax Journal*, vol. 13 (March 1960), pp. 1–16; and Martha Derthick, *The Influence of Federal Grants: Public Assistance in Massachusetts* (Harvard University Press, 1970).

19. On the politics of the Great Society programs see James L. Sundquist, *Politics and Policy: The Eisenhower, Kennedy, and Johnson Years* (Brookings Institution, 1968).

the poor were entrapped at an early age, and which could be broken and thus prevented by a well-coordinated series of specific social services. Entitlements, formula grants, and project grants differed in many respects, but they generally shared this common political foundation: program categories grew step-by-step with newly perceived categories of deserving need.

This approach puzzles those who are insensitive to its deep normative roots. If people are poor, the logical and efficient course is simply to give them money, thus doing away with demeaning income tests, armies of social workers, and other ills inherent in a categorical welfare establishment.[20] The United States has repeatedly considered such approaches—negative income taxes, guaranteed annual incomes, family assistance plans, and variants on these themes—and has repeatedly rejected them. The reasons are essentially normative: liberals and conservatives have never agreed on the just levels and cutoff points of aid for individual recipients; the proper role and design of work incentives and requirements as a precondition of aid; and the just allocation of aid among regions. Indeed, the defeat of the Nixon family assistance plan in the Senate was largely attributable to nay votes of senators of southern states whose economic interests (more money) would have been enhanced by the bill, and whose opposition can only be explained by values.[21]

Similar normative disputes beset the debate, now growing ancient, over national health insurance. The fundamental disagreement is about who is legitimately entitled to government assistance in paying medical bills and on what terms. Since enactment of medicare (elderly and, later, disabled) and medicaid (welfare poor) no value consensus has emerged on whether public health insurance should cover everyone, the rest of the poor, mothers and children, those facing catastrophically high health bills, or anyone who first pays a sizable sum of his own money. Thus it is not strange that federal policy has allowed "legitimate" entitlement programs to expand (notably medicare),[22] that new programs for new social groups have been few and

20. For instance, Milton Friedman, *Capitalism and Freedom* (University of Chicago Press, 1962), chap. 12.

21. Otto A. Davis and John E. Jackson, "Senate Defeat of the Family Assistance Plan," *Public Policy*, vol. 22 (Summer 1974), pp. 245–73.

22. In 1981 and especially in 1982, Congress made some cuts in medicare—notably increases in beneficiary deductibles and reductions in payments to doctors and hospitals—at the request of the Reagan administration. The cuts were fairly small, however, given the size and expansionary force of the program, which when the cuts were enacted was expected to double its budget within five years and soon reach insolvency in its trust fund. The major

small, or that challenges to expansion have been targeted on the question of who is deserving (the Reagan administration, for example, wanted to cap medicaid, which is presumably tainted by welfare "chiselers" and wanted to drive the working poor off the welfare rolls).

These normative considerations help explain why grant and income support programs in the United States tend to emerge categorically; but within the universe of legitimate and enacted categories, why is it so difficult to consolidate or devolve programs as administrative complexities multiply? The answer lies in several additional normative considerations that themselves involve distinctive properties of the American political system. In American federalism the central government has never been viewed as a mere aid to the states, but also and equally as a constraint on them, and as a practical matter, constraint has often widely been seen to be necessary.

Properties of American Federalism

Three features of American federalism have traditionally given cause for concern. The first is the sheer number of states. Intergovernmental relations appropriate to ten Canadian provinces or eleven German Länder cannot be easily transported to fifty states spread over a vast area and exhibiting diverse cultural preferences and historical and regional traditions. As Madison said in *Federalist 10*, under the Constitution, "the great and aggregate interests" are entrusted to the national legislature, and "the local and particular to the State legislatures."[23] The rights, entitlements, and other benefits awarded by means of federal grant-in-aid programs have at least some of the character of "great and aggregate interests" (in modern parlance, "national priorities"). They are not merely local and particular concerns, and so unfettered diversity has seemed undesirable. Because America's extreme separation of powers (which rewards legislative localism) and privatism (which deliberately shares public power with the private sector) already honor decentralization in the design and implementation of federal programs, still further steps toward diversity of welfare benefits (already absurdly uneven here by European standards) are difficult to

cost containment measure enacted in medicare—a prospective payment plan for hospitals, included in the reform of the social security program adopted early in 1983—falls on providers, who are prohibited from billing patients to recoup federal revenues lost under the new system. On balance, then, the legitimacy and political strength of the program remain intact.

23. *The Federalist Papers* (Mentor, 1961), p. 83.

defend. Nor is it easy to reconcile local autonomy with broad central guidelines in federal-state negotiating forums such as those between the central government and the provinces in Canada, which apparently work well there.[24] Where policy uniformity is desirable in the American federal system, the federal government must try to impose it. As a former social security official once explained in an interview: "You centralize so that you can raise hell with one source, not with fifty, if things go wrong."

Second, many observers—including some of the same classic sources so often quoted on the virtues of local control[25]—have repeatedly remarked on the superior capacity and efficiency of federal government officials to those at the state and local levels. Some states and localities have had a reputation for inefficiency, incapacity, and even dishonesty. Some state and local political systems have been deeply marked by machine politics based in the statehouse, courthouse, or city hall. In many, the fight against corruption has entailed depoliticizing such traditionally local functions as education and police administration, creating new local forms of fragmentation. In many areas "leadership by elected officials" has meant corruption and "politics," while "clean and honest government" has meant depriving politicians of the means of exercising leadership. If devolution mainly works to nourish political corruption or bureaucratic leadership, it is difficult to be enthusiastic about the unleashed vitality of state and local government it is alleged to produce. Of course, the states and some localities have improved, modernized, and professionalized to the point where some observers now think them "maligned."[26] But doubts remain, the most important concerning the degree to which modernization and professionalization are *products* of steady federal pressure and might be retarded in its absence.[27]

Third, some states discriminate against blacks, the poor, or other minorities—or might do so if they were left to themselves. As spokesmen for these groups generally point out whenever devolution is debated, the disadvantaged have traditionally looked to the federal government as their source of protection (albeit imperfect) against local indifference or abuse.

24. William A. Glaser, "Federalism in Canadian Health Services—Lessons for the United States" (Columbia University, Center for Social Sciences, December 1977).

25. For example, *Federalist Papers*, nos. 3 (pp. 43–45), 4 (pp. 47–48), and 27 (pp. 174–175); and de Tocqueville, *Democracy in America*, vol. 1, pp. 161, 401.

26. Ira Sharkansky, *The Maligned States: Policy Accomplishments, Problems, and Opportunities* (McGraw-Hill, 1972). See also Samuel H. Beer, "The Modernization of American Federalism," *Publius*, vol. 3 (Fall 1973), pp. 49–95.

27. On this point see Derthick, *The Influence of Federal Grants*, especially chap. 8.

Some states, dominated by legislatures influenced strongly by rural interests, would discriminate against cities in allocating aid. Some might use flexible federal funds not as an addition to their own fiscal efforts but as a substitute for them. It is feared, in short, that the rationales of some programs would be defeated by large state and local discretion, and some therefore argue for tight federal strings. The state and local situation is no doubt changing, but it is not changing everywhere at a uniform rate, and little is known about the incidence and rate of change.

These three factors distinguish the U.S. government from most other federal systems with which it might be compared. Canadian and West European federal systems have many fewer subunits; more centralized, bureaucratized, and professionalized administrative systems; welfare programs with more uniform entitlements; and more manageable race relations.[28] These points are well borne in mind when it is remarked that the United States alone lacks an extensive program of federal revenues shared with subnational units. Other federal systems, unlike that of the United States, generally honor the maxim that one must first centralize in order to decentralize effectively.

In short, opposition to devolution has traditionally rested on three normative grounds: philosophical (federally raised money should be spent for purposes deemed proper by the federal government); efficiency (states and cities might not use shared revenue productively and might cut back their own efforts if string-free federal funds became available); and distributional (states and localities might discriminate against minorities or politically weak constituents).

Proponents of devolution have countered by trying to show that these issues are no longer weighty, and that if they remain, devolution offers benefits that more than offset the costs it might carry. On philosophical grounds, they have argued that the size of the federal system is a reason for, not against, devolution: efforts at federal control of fifty states addressing social problems in highly distinct contexts must generate arbitrary requirements and unresponsive programs. They have argued further that categorical programs nourish federal bureaucratic power at the expense of elected state and local generalist officials, an unhealthy and undemocratic development. On efficiency grounds they have insisted that state and local

28. See Christopher Leman, *The Collapse of Welfare Reform: Political Institutions, Policy, and the Poor in Canada and the United States* (MIT Press, 1980); and Arnold J. Heidenheimer and others, *Comparative Public Policy: The Politics of Social Choice in Europe and America*, 2d ed. (St. Martin's, 1983).

capacities have improved greatly of late and that learning through doing is basic to continued improvement and vitality. On distributional grounds they have insisted that racial discrimination and antiurban bias are far less common than in the past, and that lingering discrimination could be prevented by simple, minimal federal requirements and enforcement of existing civil rights laws.

In short, devolution proposals have been perceived and debated in a normative context with compelling arguments on both sides. These value perceptions shaped the "standing decisions"[29] and initial negotiating positions of the participants in the political debate. As the grant-in-aid system grew and the political context of intergovernmental relations changed, these issues were joined with renewed force in the 1970s when the Nixon administration determined to press for wide-ranging devolution.

Approaches to Devolution

Among the major obstacles to devolution have been the weight the arguments against it have been thought to carry and the political unity of those impressed by one or more of these opposing arguments. An equally important obstacle has been the customary inability of devolution proponents to agree on what they want. Several different schools of thought may be isolated.

1. Substituters. To some, the essence of devolution is to transform several categorical grants into one broader package at existing or reduced levels of federal funding or to turn over a portion of federal tax revenues in exchange for the demise of categorical programs. Substitution appeals strongly to fiscal conservatives, of course.

2. Supplementers. To others, devolution means either new string-free programs in addition to existing grants-in-aid or a consolidation of programs given additional money. Liberals are especially drawn to this image.[30]

3. Decentralizers. To still others, devolution is mainly a means of reducing the power of the federal government in state and local affairs. Whether more or less federal money is spent in achieving this end is irrelevant.

4. Consolidators. Devolution may promise greater administrative ef-

29. The term is taken from V.O. Key, Jr., and Frank Munger, "Social Determinism and Electoral Decision: The Case of Indiana," in Frank Munger and Douglas Price, eds., *Readings in Political Parties and Pressure Groups* (Crowell, 1964), p. 370.

30. On these orientations in the general revenue-sharing debate, see Dommel, *The Politics of Revenue Sharing*, especially chaps. 3 and 4.

ficiency and rationality by combining several fragmented programs into one or a smaller number. The consolidated program might be subject to tight federal strings (that is, it need not be highly decentralized) and it might be funded at either a higher or lower level than its components had before. The heart of this orientation is administrative rationalization.

5. Equalizers. Some proponents have viewed devolution as a means of improving interjurisdictional equity. Aid (new or repackaged) might be allocated by a formula favoring state and local governments whose fiscal capacity (tax base) is small in relation to the size and needs of their population. Redress of regional inequality is the essence of this conception.[31]

It is clear that devolution means different things to different people, that there is no unified agenda shared by devolution proponents, and indeed that some versions of the approach are inconsistent with others. When the internal division of the proponents is set alongside the powerful normative arguments of the opponents, the bases of inaction become clearer and the mystery of enactment of the three programs in the early 1970s becomes still more intriguing.

Values: Successes and Failures

Given the normative context of the devolution issue, one might logically expect two conditions of change: weakening agreement within the forces of opposition and increasing agreement among devolution proponents— in other words, collapse of the opposing coalition and a newly cemented coalition among advocates. In the success cases these conditions occurred; in the failures they did not. To understand the differences one must look in more detail at value considerations, the political structures within which change was considered, and the political strategies by which coalition building was pursued.

One key to the enactment of the successful devolution initiatives was the value orientation of President Richard M. Nixon (and of many top political executives under him). In the categories set out above, Nixon is best described as a "decentralizer." This orientation proved to be conducive to coalition building because it gave him both the ideological ardor to persist and the fiscal flexibility to bargain with devolution proponents of other persuasions. Less committed politicians might have hesitated before

31. Beer, "The Adoption of General Revenue Sharing," p. 138.

the opponents' philosophical, efficiency, and distributional concerns, but Nixon's values immunized him against such doubts. Nixon had a profoundly bitter distaste not only for the federal bureaucracy but for the entire federal "establishment." He was convinced that these constellations of congressional committees, executive agencies, and interest groups had sustained a steady encroachment of the federal government on subnational and private prerogatives, and he was determined to defeat them.[32]

To Nixon and other committed decentralizers, the quality, efficiency, and equity of state and local government were peripheral issues. To them, the benefits of decentralization outweighed the costs it might entail; indeed, to the more fervent among them, the performance of state and local government was a priori immaterial, for however bad such subnational performance might be, federal performance must necessarily be worse. To the dedicated decentralizer, striking a blow against the federal government is virtually an end in itself; whether doing so would cost more or less money is beside the point. Thus a strong decentralizer would be, as Nixon was and as fiscal conservatives were not, quite content to increase the federal budgets for revenue-sharing and block grant programs if such a step would increase their chance of enactment.[33] As will be seen, the legislative successes did indeed come to rest on a coalition of largely conservative decentralizers and largely liberal supplementers.

Successes

It is convenient to consider the two later successes—CETA (1973) and CDBG (1974)—and then return to examine the first of the three—general

32. Asked in a press conference of February 17, 1971, whether he was disappointed by Congress's reaction to his revenue-sharing plans, Nixon replied that he was not, that all reforms have "rough sledding." He described the opponents of reform as "the establishment . . . the establishment of Congress, the establishment of the Federal bureaucracy, and also great organizations, labor organizations, farm organizations, business organizations [that] have all gotten used to dealing with government as it is and they are always afraid of change. . . ." He went on to contrast Washington, "the very summit of government," and its "dug-in establishmentarians fighting for the status quo . . ." with "down in the valleys, where the people live," where "the people in the frontline, the leaders in the frontlines, the Governors, the mayors, the county officials, an overwhelming majority of them are for revenue sharing . . . and also an overwhelming majority of the people of this country are for revenue sharing. . . ." *Public Papers of the Presidents: Richard Nixon,1971* (GPO, 1972), p. 167. (Hereafter *Public Papers: Nixon, 1971*.)

33. On the making of these legislative initiatives, see Nathan and Calkins, "The Story of Revenue Sharing," pp. 20–23.

revenue sharing (1972)—against this background. The manpower and urban development programs were at the heart of the growing crisis of urban liberalism in the late 1960s and early 1970s. After high hopes for a war on poverty in the Kennedy administration and the launching of this war among other Great Society programs in Lyndon Johnson's administration, the entire federal antipoverty effort came under sharp attack in the late 1960s. Among many sources of friction and disillusion, several stood out. First, activists in community action agencies, model cities offices, and elsewhere, encouraged by federal citizen participation requirements, made life difficult for mayors and other local officials.[34] The extent of these conflicts may have been exaggerated—apparently most community action agencies were far less inclined toward battling city hall than were a few worst cases[35]—but they were very well publicized. Second, the programs failed to buy the social peace many had anticipated. Recurrent urban riots, the rise of black nationalist and separatist sentiment, and the spread of black power and general antiwhite feeling in spite of—indeed seemingly in direct proportion to—federal program building disabused early optimists of the view that federal demonstrations of social concern and compassion would solve the race problem. Third, the programs were vulnerable to many questions of logic, efficiency, and effectiveness. Edward C. Banfield and other critics pressed penetrating and skeptical arguments questioning whether the programs could ever work,[36] and the folly of "throwing money at problems" came to be a cliché. Fourth, scandals arose often enough, especially in the subsidized housing programs, to put the antipoverty effort in general ill repute. Most of these problems were highly visible by the late 1960s. The 1970s brought more of the same and with it new neoconservative critiques. Concern grew over the integrity and vitality of local government beset by federally encouraged "guerrillas"; about the protection of social order against rioters and agitators thought to be encouraged by federal rhetoric; about the need for reduced expectations, milder public discourse, and recognition of the limits of federally induced behavioral and cultural change; and about the need for greater honesty and efficiency in implementation and administration of grant programs.

34. Daniel P. Moynihan, *Maximum Feasible Misunderstanding: Community Action in the War on Poverty* (Free Press, 1969).

35. John H. Strange, "Community Action in North Carolina: Maximum Feasible Misunderstanding? Mistake? Or Magic Formula?" *Publius*, vol. 2 (Fall 1972), pp. 51–73.

36. Edward C. Banfield, *The Unheavenly City: The Nature and Future of Our Urban Crisis* (Little, Brown, 1968).

MANPOWER PROGRAMS

In the early 1970s, Nixon's decentralist zeal increasingly confronted not the traditional normative defenses of federal prerogatives but rather a disconsolate and disspirited liberalism unsure of the merits of approaches it had embraced with assurance only five years before. Even highly liberal legislators agreed that manpower programs needed reorganization, including consolidation. In 1968 a postelection task force led by George Shultz argued the case for consolidation and decentralization. The following year a national manpower policy task force of academicians offered similar arguments. Influential policy analysts, sharply critical of the fragmentation of manpower training sources and of the confusion it visited on would-be trainees, urged that training sources coordinate to create one-stop contact points at the local level.[37] A manpower training block grant came close to enactment in 1970. The major reason why CETA did not finally emerge until 1973 was not congressional opposition to block grants, but rather legislative-executive battling over the liberals' determination to attach a public service employment program to the bill and to make the administration accept it as a price of support for its own objectives.[38]

COMMUNITY DEVELOPMENT PROGRAMS

By 1972 there was a similar sense that the urban development programs were in need of revision. By this time much of the political luster of the main development program, urban renewal, had dimmed. In the 1950s and early 1960s the program had been a generously funded and highly attractive (albeit controversial) "mayor's program": in New Haven, Boston, and elsewhere, political careers were launched and downtowns rebuilt with federal renewal grants. By 1970 renewal politics had changed radically. Cities, such as Boston, that underbudgeted their projects and then repeatedly applied for large "amendatories" to finish them dramatized fiscal indiscipline in the program and spurred Nixon budget makers to tighten federal controls. The solution, heavy reliance on the "neighborhood de-

37. A pre-Nixon discussion of the need for coordination in federal and local manpower efforts is Sar A. Levitan and Garth L. Mangum, *Making Sense of Federal Manpower Policy*, Policy Papers in Human Resources and Industrial Relations, no. 2 (University of Michigan and Wayne State University: Institute of Labor and Industrial Relations, March 1967).

38. For details as of 1971, see Davidson, *The Politics of Comprehensive Manpower Legislation*.

velopment program" approach (established late in Johnson's administration), which made next year's funding levels contingent on the present year's performance, left locals fearful that ambitious undertakings would languish should federal aid be abruptly withdrawn.

The local political liabilities of the program had grown too. By the mid-1960s the program had acquired a reputation as a "federal bulldozer":[39] urban renewal, its critics charged, meant "Negro removal." In response the federal government began insisting upon such protections as the "one for one" rule, which required that a unit of housing for the poor be made available for every such unit eliminated by a renewal project, and requirements that before a project could proceed cities must devise and win approval of elaborate relocation plans for those to be displaced from their homes. And the more militant and participatory urban poor of the late 1960s, who viewed these federal responses as too little, too late, were more inclined and better equipped to block renewal plans. In sum, federal constraints, local opposition, and the program's tainted reputation combined to raise the political costs of renewal. Mayors increasingly looked elsewhere for resources with which to build their budgets and careers. As the mayors, the program's major constituency, grew distant, critics on both left and right took aim at an increasingly vulnerable target.

Model cities, the other major urban redevelopment program (it and urban renewal would comprise 90 percent of the funds in the CDBG program) was in little better shape. Since its enactment in 1966 the program had encountered protracted problems. Much time and political energy had been devoted to the mechanics of resident participation, often at the expense of planning. Mayors, expected to exert vigorous leadership in the program, and federal departments, expected to concentrate categorical grant funds under their control on the model neighborhoods, had often proved to be detached and uncooperative. Small appropriations divided among dozens of projects in each of 150 cities had only a limited impact. And a program so targeted that it reached "only" one-third of the legislative districts in the country seemed to be neither generalizable nor equitable to a Republican administration impressed by the political demography of rapidly growing Republican suburbs and counties, which argued for diffusion. On the other hand, this targeted holdover of the Johnson years was

39. *The Federal Bulldozer*, the polemical title of Martin Anderson's book on urban renewal (MIT Press, 1964), was indicative of the program's declining image.

also "one of the most important existing stepping stones to revenue sharing," having many fewer strings attached than other urban programs.[40] The administration therefore debated about the program, retained it, tinkered with it, loosened its few strings still further, and determined to phase it into a more general package of urban development legislation.

Even as urban renewal and model cities came under attack, scandals broke out in the two major subsidized housing programs (sections 235 and 236) established by the National Housing and Urban Development Act of 1968. Although these unhappy developments reflected the weakness of federal control, not its excess,[41] newspaper headlines universally left the impression that HUD had failed again, and that the feds had become the nation's largest slumlord. Liberals who had worked to create the programs found it impolitic to defend them and moved to put distance between themselves and their four-year-old progeny. Embarrassing public quarrels erupted between the House Housing Subcommittee and the full Banking and Currency Committee. Faced with chaos and confusion surrounding an omnibus housing bill in 1972, the Rules Committee declined to grant a rule and the bill died, a vivid demonstration of congressional division and indecision. Moving into the breach in January 1973, Nixon unilaterally imposed a freeze on new commitments under these programs; the move caused some outcries about executive usurpation, but they were not very loud and no one doubted that he would get away with it. These developments left the administration in a strong bargaining position: having frozen funds in tainted programs, it could insist on the changes that later were enacted in the 1974 CDBG legislation as a price of restoring the flow of funds.

In short, the passage of block grants in the manpower and urban development fields is explained by the triumph of a set of program-specific value perceptions over the general normative objectives that had traditionally held the line against devolution. Enactment of CETA and CDBG did not signal a basic change of direction, or a new normative acceptance of devolution. These victories were contingent on the coincidence of decentralist zeal in the executive and a crisis of confidence in a subset of liberal programs in two policy arenas whose features may not be widely generalizable.

40. Nixon described the program in these terms in an urban aid message to Congress on March 5, 1971, reprinted in *Public Papers: Nixon, 1971*, p. 402.

41. U.S. Commission on Civil Rights, *Home Ownership for Lower Income Families: A Report on the Racial and Ethnic Impact of the Section 235 Program* (GPO, June 1971).

GENERAL REVENUE SHARING

These value considerations are also of major explanatory importance for the first devolution success, the State and Local Fiscal Assistance Act of 1972. Unlike manpower and community development, general revenue sharing imposed no consolidation or rearrangement. It simply created a new unrestricted program of aid to state and local governments. It involved no distinct policy arenas with distinct political properties. An adequate explanation begins with the peculiar coincidence of fiscal perceptions and political values in the early 1970s.

By 1972 it was widely believed that state and local governments were suffering from an acute, worsening fiscal crisis. Some observers argued that inflation had replaced rioting as the new terror of the cities. For reasons that are still not entirely clear, the costs of running local governments rose much faster than the general rate of inflation.[42] Costs of everything soared, from teachers' salaries in the largest cities to the asphalt with which to repave the smallest village street, and the need for immediate and sizable fiscal relief was widely accepted.

Relief could have taken many forms, of course, including new or enlarged federal categorical programs or newly federalized welfare programs. This approach was unacceptable for three major reasons. First, Nixon, the Republican decentralizer, controlled the White House and therewith a major portion of the federal agenda. In 1969, persuaded that a larger federal role in income support programs was important to an orderly sorting out of functions in the federal system, Nixon had proposed a federally funded family assistance plan, part of whose appeal was a consolidation of narrow categorical welfare programs, thought to be partly to blame for the much-discussed welfare "mess." The depth of the president's commitment to the proposal is unclear, however; certainly it diminished when it hit rough sledding in Congress.[43] General revenue sharing also had been near the top of the list of New Federalism proposals since the administration took office in 1969, but unlike the family assistance plan, it remained there.

42. In 1971 Norton Long noted, "Over the last decade there has been a 54 percent inflation of state and local government costs (compared to 23 percent in the private sector)." "The City as Reservation," *The Public Interest*, no. 25 (Fall 1971), p. 25.

43. There is a large literature on the family assistance plan, with much concern for and controversy over blame-fixing for its death. The question cannot be examined here. See, among other sources, Daniel P. Moynihan, *The Politics of a Guaranteed Income: The Nixon Administration and the Family Assistance Plan* (Random House, 1973); and Vincent J. Burke and Vee Burke, *Nixon's Good Deed: Welfare Reform* (Columbia University Press, 1974).

Second, the crisis of urban liberalism left the usual defenders of the categorical approach reluctant to urge it as a general solution to the needs of the states and localities. (By 1972 liberals too agreed that a federalized welfare system was dead politically.) Third, the case for general aid was pressed by an intergovernmental lobby of state, county, and local officials, who had sharpened their political teeth on the Great Society programs and were determined to secure more aid on more favorable (that is, less restricted) terms.[44]

Nixon's $1 billion general revenue-sharing proposal of 1969 met with little enthusiasm in Congress or in the intergovernmental lobby. By 1971 it was clear both that Nixon needed this lobby to exert pressure on Congress and that the lobby would do so only if the financial rewards were greatly enlarged. Nixon responded by raising the ante to a $5 billion program, and the lobby's interest and activism grew impressively. Stepping up its efforts on the Hill, the lobby found congressmen increasingly afraid not to grant fiscal relief, lest their unwillingness work for their local opponents.[45] This consideration may well have been of particular interest to House Ways and Means Committee chairman Wilbur Mills, Democrat of Arkansas, until then the staunchest and most effective congressional opponent of revenue sharing, when he declared his candidacy for the 1972 Democratic presidential nomination and began listening sympathetically to the plaints of local party notables.

The case for general revenue sharing fit the conventional wisdom of the day. For several years the Advisory Commission on Intergovernmental Relations and academic experts had been arguing that narrowly drawn categorical aid strengthened the hand of functional specialists in public agencies throughout the federal system at the expense of political generalists. Moreover, the fiscal crisis centered on the costs incurred by generalist officials in performing the routine functions of general-purpose governments. It seemed only logical and fitting that the federal government should respond with general aid to general officials for general governmental functions, that is, with a program of general revenue sharing. The traditional view would have argued that federal aid should be extended only to legitimate and delimited categories of need, but few felt confident to define and defend such programmatic categories in the aftermath of the Great Society and in the climate of the early 1970s.

44. Beer, "The Adoption of General Revenue Sharing," pp. 158–71.
45. Nathan and Calkins, "The Story of General Revenue Sharing," pp. 27, 30–31.

Failures

In the cases of the four failures—education, law enforcement, transportation, and rural development—the value context was very different and far less conducive to devolution. The administration badly wanted education block grants, to take the most important case, and the federal role in education had come in for skepticism and criticism in what had become a sizable body of literature by 1970. The policy implications of this new viewpoint were unclear and hardly supportive of devolution, however.

The most important element of the old conventional wisdom—that the surest route to improved pupil achievement was higher public spending on schools and teachers—had received a rude rebuff in a report, *Equality of Educational Opportunity*, prepared by sociologist James S. Coleman and colleagues in 1966.[46] The central finding of this long and complex study was that the obstacles to improved achievement by the disadvantaged had less to do with school attributes than with family background, meaning influences in the home that affected the child's attitudes toward education and sense of personal capacity. These findings gave no encouragement to those hoping to expand the federal role in the nation's school systems, but neither did they bolster the arguments of devolution proponents. To Daniel Moynihan, a top adviser in the Nixon White House, and a social scientist who had studied the Coleman findings closely, the report argued for caution among policymakers and for more academic research.[47] Indeed, in some quarters one of the report's key findings—that pupils at lower socioeconomic levels achieved more when placed in classrooms with higher-status fellows—seemed to argue for policies to overcome the class and racial separation sustained by the prevailing system of neighborhood schools. This course was incompatible with devolution, and indeed by the early 1970s the federal courts were busy imposing busing and metropolitan desegregation plans on angry localities.

The growing body of research on the implementation of compensatory education programs was no more supportive of devolution than was the research on the correlates of pupil achievement. The literature on state

46. James S. Coleman and associates, *Equality of Educational Opportunity* (GPO, 1966).
47. On the climate of policymaking for education within the executive branch at this time, see Chester E. Finn, *Education and the Presidency* (Lexington Books, 1977). For Moynihan's reflections on the Coleman report, see Daniel P. Moynihan, *Coping: On the Practice of Government* (Random House, 1973), pp. 167–84.

and local administration of title I of the Elementary and Secondary Education Act of 1965 seemed to favor more federal strings, not fewer. Reviewing the first years of the ESEA in 1968, Bailey and Mosher found that implementation was highly uneven and they were sharply critical of the revenue-sharing alternative.[48] In the early 1970s Jerome Murphy described in detail how the objective of title I—to concentrate new federal funds on innovative techniques addressed to the most disadvantaged pupils in the most disadvantaged school systems—had been thwarted by local officials who preferred to use the new funds to support general and routine school functions, and how timid federal and state officials, although aware of the distortion, did little to stop it.[49]

In short, the prevalent critique of the federal role in education maintained that the locals, given excessive discretion by the federal government, had undercut program goals and would undercut them still further if given greater discretion. This local-centered diagnosis contrasted sharply with the federal-centered critiques generally accepted in the urban development and manpower fields, and with the generalist views so supportive of general revenue sharing. This diagnosis gave confidence to opponents of education revenue sharing, who advanced their normative arguments with a tenacity quite lacking among categorical proponents in these other fields.

The three other "failed" policy areas also lacked a critique persuasively supportive of the case for devolution, a fact apparently evident even to the administration itself, which made no major effort to win enactment of its special revenue-sharing proposals in these fields. Like education, transportation policy was the subject of intensely critical discussion in the early 1970s, but most participants agreed that the central issues were broad questions of *national* policy priorities, especially the relative emphasis between highways and mass transit, to which revenue sharing (and indeed the whole subject of intergovernmental relations) was largely secondary. Law enforcement revenue sharing, which, an official later recalled, added a few programs to the Law Enforcement Assistance Administration in order to make the list of block grants look "blockier," would have expanded a program that had encountered many problems since its enactment in 1968.[50]

48. Stephen K. Bailey and Edith K. Mosher, *ESEA: The Office of Education Administers a Law* (Syracuse University Press, 1968), especially pp. 187–204, 213–28.

49. Jerome T. Murphy, "The Education Bureaucracies Implement Novel Policy: The Politics of Title I of ESEA, 1965–72," in Allan Sindler, ed., *Policy and Politics in America: Six Case Studies* (Little, Brown, 1973), pp. 161–98.

50. *Block Grant Programs of the Law Enforcement Assistance Administration*, H. Rept. 1072, 92 Cong. 2 sess. (GPO, 1972).

Finally, few believed that the iron hand of the federal government was an important problem in rural development policy, or that devolution in that field was worth much intellectual or political energy.

Structure: Successes and Failures

The value orientations and perceptions of participants in the debate about devolution proposals are basic to understanding outcomes, but they are not the whole story. Public and private actors entertain their thoughts and advance their views in institutions with norms, customs, limits, prerogatives, and stakes of their own, and these elements of public and private power structure do much to determine whether actors with given value positions will advance, change, or repress their views.

In the politics of devolution, structural variables were important in three ways. First, the structural separation of powers in American government raises obstacles to innovation by allowing one political party to hold the White House while the other holds a majority in the Congress. Throughout Nixon's presidency (1969–74), both House and Senate had sizable Democratic majorities, some of whose members had considerable personal, partisan, and policy distaste for the administration and were skeptical about or hostile to devolution. In such a setting the support of relevant congressional committees is crucial. A supportive committee might or might not be able to persuade a majority of the members in its chamber to endorse a policy departure proposed by an executive of the other political party, but such a majority has almost no chance of forming when committees are strongly opposed. For this reason the values and beliefs of key committee members gained special importance, and these values and beliefs were shaped in part by legislative roles, including the wish for "credit claiming" and other rewards supportive of the legislative career,[51] the sense of patrimony and proprietorship in programs, and the sense of pride in legislative craft.

Second, because a Republican executive in favor of devolution confronted a skeptical Democratic Congress, major interest groups in the public and private sectors might hold the balance of power. The executive might ally with powerful groups in hopes of battling Congress into submission. Conversely, a phalanx of legislators and interests arrayed in

51. David R. Mayhew, *Congress: The Electoral Connection* (Yale University Press, 1974).

opposition might decisively stymie the executive's plans. One should therefore examine group stakes in devolution and the structure of group-government relations in the programs to be devolved.

Third, because devolution shifts responsibilities among levels of the federal system, the political consequences of such a shift, especially for Congress and for the interested groups, must be considered. Some groups fare better at some levels of the federal system than at others. Whatever the abstract case for devolution, the distinctive interplay between policy arenas and the political systems of different levels of the federal system generates disagreements of value and interest.

Failures

The structural politics of the four failure cases may be captured in the following generalization: legislators convinced of the value of categorical programs (or of the pitfalls of block grants) opposed devolution in concert with powerful interest groups that were strongly distrustful of program consolidation at the state level. This generalization will be defended in a brief review of three of the four failures.[52]

RURAL DEVELOPMENT

Nixon's proposal for rural development revenue sharing would have consolidated eleven categorical programs into one lump sum allocated to the states (that is, governors and legislators). These programs were in no sense in crisis: congressmen and rural interests alike had a high opinion of both the older ones (for example, the Cooperative Extension Service, created in 1914) and the newer (for instance, the Economic Development Act and the Appalachian Regional Commission, begun in the 1960s). Some were viewed as highly successful farmers' programs, others as small, overdue federal commitments to an otherwise neglected rural America. The legislative strategy was simple: in the Senate (on which the discussion here will focus) Hubert Humphrey, Democrat of Minnesota, chairman of the Rural Development Subcommittee of the Committee on Agriculture and Forestry, made it clear that he was skeptical of revenue sharing ("gravely

52. The administration's transportation proposals, dismissed by Congress so peremptorily that neither House nor Senate held hearings on them, add little analytically to the other cases and so will not be treated here. On transportation revenue sharing, which "generated so little attention and support that it simply faded quietly away," see Conlon, "Congressional Response to the New Federalism," chap. 6.

concerned") but broad-minded (not "adamantly opposed"),[53] and then sat back to listen as a long parade of interest groups told the legislators of the virtues of their programs and the dangers of devolution.

Spokesmen for the National Association of State Universities and Land Grant Colleges, the Appalachian Regional Commission, and the National Association of Development Organizations all stoutly defended existing programs and urged that they continue to receive separate funds. They spoke against "simply redistributing the money" under revenue sharing, and one declared that "there are many areas of revenue sharing that really frighten rural America." The chief forester of the American Forestry Association, terming the proposal "a ticket to confusion and disaster," said "we have not received one letter in support" of it from the group's 83,000 members. Officials of the National Association of Farmer Elected Committeemen and the National Association of Conservation Districts added their groups' opposition to rural revenue sharing and their support for existing programs "which are functioning successfully and contributing to the public good." The legislative representative of the National Rural Electric Cooperative Association called the plan "a serious setback to rural development." A nineteen-member National Coalition of Farm and Commodity Organizations was strongly opposed. Under the administration plan, the group's president noted, governors could use consolidated grant funds as matching shares of other categorical programs, such as hospital construction, or could use them to attract industry by constructing roads or for various other uses the farmers thought inappropriate. The National Grange, one of the coalition's most prominent members, declared on its own behalf that it would not "stand idly by and see good programs destroyed because farmers do not have the political clout to control the expenditures of the funds for rural development within their States or local governments." Even the American Farm Bureau Federation, which mentioned its official support of the plan, added that "we are not putting on any great campaign" for it.[54]

In the course of deploring the administration's plan, the legislators and interest group spokesmen developed three main themes. First, participants in federal-rural relations were by and large quite content with the categorical system. The witnesses did not view themselves as victims of federal bu-

53. *Rural Development*, Hearings before the Subcommittee on Rural Development of the Senate Committee on Agriculture and Forestry, 92 Cong. 1 sess. (GPO, 1971), pt. 2, p. 32.

54. Ibid., pp. 59, 120–24, 149, 165, and pt. 6, pp. 34, 51, 60, 75, 80, 82.

reaucratic dictation. Most emphasized the pervasive localism of their programs, the extensive participation of grassroots elements. Most looked on the Department of Agriculture as a valued protector of the farmers' interests. There were frictions with the department, to be sure, but spokesmen agreed that the sensible response was to improve the workings of the department, not to remove its control of programs by means of revenue sharing, and still less to eliminate it altogether in a reorganized "superdepartment," as the administration had also proposed.

Second, there was overwhelming agreement that rural categoricals ought not to lose their programmatic identity by being merged and made dependent for funding and even survival on the shifting tides of state politics. Rural needs were invisible and of low priority in many statehouses, witnesses agreed, and Humphrey remarked repeatedly and sardonically on the absence of television cameras from the hearing room. The hearings betrayed a sense that rural America had been shunted aside in favor of the cities, whose problems, ironically, were in large part the product of flight from rural areas that had been allowed to decline. Federal abandonment of rural interests to urban-dominated statehouses and legislatures by means of revenue sharing therefore had powerful symbolic as well as material importance.

Third, the witnesses again and again recorded their indignation that the administration was discussing a rearrangement of modest funds among governments when it was clear to all that "rural America needs everything"—housing, roads, health care, schools, jobs, industry, plumbing, and on and on. The "ballgame," Humphrey declared, was economic development and jobs; and he was determined not "to get this committee just bound up in the battle over special revenue sharing and forget what the ballgame is about."[55]

The administration's plan awakened little enthusiasm within the subcommittee itself. Most of the questioning was conducted by Humphrey and Senator James Allen, Democrat of Alabama, who on many issues stood at opposite ideological poles in the Democratic party. On the revenue-sharing question Allen was more laconic but no less skeptical than Humphrey. Republicans seldom took part in the colloquies and had little good to say for the administration's plan when they did. The legislators were generally content to sit back, swap stories and memories of small-town life

55. Ibid., pt. 2, p. 36.

with their witnesses, and let the organizations pick the administration's plan to pieces.

In its report, the Senate committee retained the categoricals intact—they were "tried and proven," it said—and at higher funding levels.[56] It authorized several new programs and established a new farm credit system, later enacted in modified form in the Rural Development Act of 1972. It made an ironic bow to revenue sharing: in addition to the retained, enlarged categoricals and its new programs, it authorized $500 million per year in new "revenue-sharing" aid for rural purposes, allocating one-third each to multijurisdictional agencies, counties, and states. This provision died in conference, for the House committee had not endorsed revenue sharing in any form. Indeed its report disdained even to acknowledge it. The committee wrote that it had faced "the option of either creating a new Federal bureaucracy or expanding the roles of existing Federal agencies," and that it had chosen the latter course.[57]

EDUCATION

In essentials, the politics of education revenue sharing were the same as those of rural development. The House Education and Labor Committee and the Senate Labor and Public Welfare committees were dominated by liberal Democrats with strong paternal concern for most of the thirty-odd categoricals the Nixon plan would consolidate under state control. Whereas Humphrey was merely "gravely concerned" about rural revenue sharing, however, House Education Subcommittee chairman Carl Perkins, Democrat of Kentucky, said flatly that the education plan was "bad news" which "alarmed" him, and Lloyd Meeds, Democrat of Washington, declared that he was "committed to fighting to the death on this issue."[58] Republicans were so reluctant to be identified with the measure that by 1973 the administration had difficulty finding a sponsor.[59]

In education, as in rural development revenue sharing, an indignant platoon of interest group spokesmen came before the committee to defend

56. *Rural Development Act of 1972*, S. Rept. 734, 92 Cong. 2 sess. (GPO, 1972), pp. 46–47.

57. *Rural Development Act of 1972*, H. Rept. 835, 92 Cong. 2 sess. (GPO, 1972), p. 1.

58. *Elementary and Secondary Education Amendments of 1973*, Hearings before the General Subcommittee on Education of the House Committee on Education and Labor, 93 Cong. 1 sess. (GPO, 1973), pp. 117–18.

59. See the sarcastic remarks of Rep. William Ford, Democrat of Michigan, in ibid., pp. 2036–37; also Orfield, *Congressional Power*, p. 167.

the categoricals and blast the administration. The National Education Association, with 1.2 million members, led the assault: "We find it unrealistic to combine existing grant programs into groupings for administrative convenience rather than for soundness in solving educational problems." The Legislative Conference of National Organizations (the so-called Big Six) supported "the stated aims" of the plan, but disagreed with its particulars. The council would not support a revenue-sharing plan that did not call for an increased federal share of education costs, and it wanted the legislation to name the chief state school officers as administrators of the funds.[60] Smaller groups then proceeded to defend the programmatic integrity of the ESEA title III, the library programs, and more.

The education groups delivered the same three messages as did their farm and conservation counterparts in connection with rural revenue sharing. First, far from compromising local control, the categorical system enhanced it. In a dialogue between Meeds and Richard Gousha, vice-president of the Council of Great City Schools, Meeds asked which gave more local control: a program administered by the federal government "where the money goes to the local school district on a formula basis" or one in which "money goes from the Federal Government to the State government to the local government and the programs to be followed by the . . . local school districts are prescribed and proscribed by the State." Gousha replied, "I think I would be inclined, Mr. Meeds, to go with the first. . . . As a city school system superintendent, I believe we would have input in the development of those guidelines which would reflect more nearly my urban interests in terms of the national goals." Meeds responded, "So when some people speak of local control and they really mean State control, it may not be as local as programs directed by the Federal Government," and Gousha agreed with that assessment.[61]

Second, the educators contended that consolidating categoricals under the control of governors would destroy the central virtues of the federal programs. In the United States, funding of education, heavily dependent on local property tax bases, is highly regressive and unequal: the poor, who need more educational services, get less. Federal programs inject an element of equalization, but do so only because they are targeted. The educators argued that consolidating these programs into one large sum at the discretion of state politicians would turn federal education funds into

60. *Elementary and Secondary Education Amendments of 1973*, Hearings, pp. 120, 152.
61. Ibid., pp. 409–10.

a "political volleyball"[62] and would probably spell the end of targeting to the disadvantaged. The state superintendent of instruction in Michigan explained that half the money allotted to his state under title I was going to Detroit. He continued, "Under revenue sharing whether or not half of that money could be allocated to Detroit, which has only 15 percent of the students of the State, is one of the pitfalls that I am saying we need to caution against. We happen to believe that Detroit needs these funds."[63]

Third, the groups made it clear that for education, as for rural America, the ballgame was money. An NEA spokesman explained his organization's opposition to revenue sharing: "We have reason to fear a loss of revenue for education programs under the special revenue sharing program. It is just that simple."[64] The education lobbies had fought long and hard for federal aid to education, scoring with passage of the ESEA in 1965 what they hoped would be only the first in a series of victories. Within five years they were fighting reductions in education spending proposed by the Nixon administration and even vetoes of education appropriation bills. Their bitter response is illustrated by an education official in New York state who complained that the administration's formula would be "financially disastrous for New York," and who made it clear that the only revenues he cared to share were growing ones: "It is true that New York would be 'saved harmless' from loss of funds . . . but we would never begin to share in the growth of the program until there is a national increase of more than $1 billion. That is not our idea of 'shared' revenues."[65]

To be sure, the education committee members were troubled by problems in implementing title I and by the perplexing research findings then accumulating on the correlates of pupil achievement. They were in no way abashed or inclined to retreat, however. The Coleman research, published in 1966, came too soon to catch the effects of title I and other major compensatory education efforts, after all, and in any case, the federal programs were modest contributions to innovation and equalization that could hardly be expected to have dramatic short-term effects on achievement. The answer to abuses in title I was a joint effort by educators, legislators, and administrators to improve federal monitoring procedures

62. Ibid., p. 164.
63. Ibid., p. 217.
64. Ibid., p. 133.
65. *Needs of Elementary and Secondary Education for the Seventies–1971*, Hearings before the General Subcommittee on Education of the House Committee on Education and Labor, 92 Cong. 1 sess. (GPO, 1971), p. 215.

and guidelines, not to open the door to further abuse by eliminating the federal role. As an AFL-CIO spokesman remarked: "If some funds from Title I are used improperly under current regulations we wonder how we could expect improvement if there are no enforceable regulations on the national level."[66]

The groups wanted protection, extension, and expansion of the ESEA and the other educational categoricals. Dismissing revenue sharing, the committees cheerfully concurred.

LAW ENFORCEMENT

Though basically consistent with the other failure cases, the politics of law enforcement revenue sharing offer several variations. Subcommittee No. 5 of the House Judiciary Committee, headed by Peter Rodino, Democrat of New Jersey, and the Subcommittee on Criminal Laws and Procedures of the Senate Judiciary Committee, chaired by John McClellan, Democrat of Arkansas, considered law enforcement revenue sharing in the context of extension of the Law Enforcement Assistance Administration, a block grant program enacted in 1968. Rural development and education revenue sharing were alternatives to categoricals that were widely thought to be working well, or mainly in need of firmer federal commitment to realize their potential. Law enforcement revenue sharing was an alternative to the political equivalent of a successful categorical: a block grant widely thought to be working poorly.

Since enactment in 1968 the block grant provisions of the LEAA had been generously funded: by one count, these funds had increased between fiscal years 1969 and 1972 from about $25 million to more than $400 million.[67] Unfortunately, the program's problems seemed to grow in proportion to its funding. The House Government Operations Committee's Subcommittee on Legal and Monetary Affairs, chaired by John S. Monagan, Democrat of Connecticut, investigated the program in 1971 and heard a long list of disturbing allegations. Some states had been slow to organize for the program and substantial sums were left unspent. It was charged

66. *Elementary and Secondary Education Amendments of 1973*, Hearings, p. 164.

67. *The Block Grant Programs of the Law Enforcement Assistance Administration*, Hearings before a Subcommittee of the House Committee on Government Operations, 92 Cong. 1 sess. (GPO, 1971), pt. 1, p. 2. On the LEAA's origins and problems, see also Thomas E. Cronin, "The War on Crime and Unsafe Streets, 1960–76: Policymaking for a Just and Safe Society," in Allan P. Sindler, ed., *America in the Seventies: Problems, Policies, and Politics* (Little, Brown, 1977), pp. 208–59.

that money had been used wastefully on consultants and on law enforcement hardware. Innovation had been less than expected and auditing had often been poor. The attorney general of Alabama charged that in his state "a law enforcement officer's dream for badly needed help was becoming merely a politician's dream for the biggest pork barrel of them all."[68] Not all states were mismanaging the program, of course, but the difficulties were numerous enough and the allegations serious enough to make the legislators wary of folding well-regarded categoricals, especially the corrections and law enforcement education programs, into a broader package along with the LEAA.

The debate about reauthorization of the LEAA in 1973 put all participants in an awkward position. Arguing the case for revenue sharing, Richard Kleindienst, attorney general in an administration that lost no opportunity to deride Great Society programs that did not work, was obliged to gloss over the problems of the LEAA, one of the weaker creations of the Johnson years, simply because it was a block grant. Kleindienst's "incredible" testimony (in the words of one legislator)[69] might be dismissed out of hand, but spokesmen for the states and localities could not be. These participants knew that the LEAA had serious problems, but they liked this new source of flexible federal money and did not want to see it eliminated or restricted. They therefore argued that the program had done much good in many states and localities and that its administration, admittedly poor in some places, was generally improving.

Unlike those who spoke on behalf of rural and education revenue sharing, generalist officials of state and local government were the main interest group spokesmen on law enforcement. The issue engaged no powerful private client groups, as did rural development, and no powerful public professional groups, as did education. Moreover, and again unlike the rural and education cases, these major interest groups split. The states favored the administration's revenue-sharing plan, which would enlarge their control over the LEAA and eliminate the requirement that they contribute matching funds. The cities endorsed the general principles of the administration's plan, but found fault with its specifics: it did not "alleviate the problems of State-to-local fund flow," did not "speak to the need for a direct role for local governments," and did not "fully address itself to the needed improvements of the State's management capabilities." The cities,

68. Ibid., p. 6.
69. *Law Enforcement Assistance Administration*, Hearings before Subcommittee No. 5 of the House Committee on the Judiciary, 93 Cong. 1 sess. (GPO, 1973), p. 94.

in short, sought "a full partnership of local government."[70] And the big cities were strongly drawn to a rival bill authored by Democrats James Stanton and John Seiberling of Ohio, which would end the "thin dew dropping of funds without concern to the areas of crime"[71] by targeting LEAA funds to the high-crime big cities.

In essence the Rodino subcommittee was obliged to choose among three options: the administration's revenue-sharing proposal, endorsed by the states but opposed by the cities; various proposals, urged by the cities, but opposed by the states, to enhance the local role in the partnership and perhaps to concentrate funds on large urban areas; and the extension, with modifications, of a block grant that had questionable merit but that no one wanted to end. As might be expected, the committee chose the third option—a careful middle-course compromise. Its report declared that it had "rejected proposals to convert this program into a simple 'no strings attached' special revenue sharing program . . . and in so doing has retained Federal responsibility for administering the program."[72] In extending the LEAA, the committee tried to please all sides: for the states, it rejected targeting proposals and reduced their matching share, and for the cities, it dismissed revenue sharing and declined to enlarge the state role. For the liberals, it expanded the LEAA's mandate from a concern with mere law enforcement to a broader focus on the criminal justice system, and it enlarged the popular law enforcement education program. And for the program's many critics everywhere, it tightened guidelines and standards in hopes of improving management and avoiding further abuses. The Senate, which considered the extension of the LEAA in haste and in much less detail, complied.

Successes

The structural politics of the three success stories may be captured as follows: The legislators who acceded to them avoided close personal association with discredited or troubled categoricals that formed only a portion of their committee agendas. The successful devolution proposals were strongly supported by lobbies of generalist public officials, and these proposals raised no major threat of state control.

70. Ibid., p. 226.
71. Ibid., p. 101.
72. *Law Enforcement Assistance Amendments*, H. Rept. 249, 93 Cong. 1 sess. (GPO, 1973), p. 5.

GENERAL REVENUE SHARING

General revenue-sharing politics fit the above generalization *mutatis mutandis*. The administration's proposal did not involve consolidation of categoricals; general revenue sharing would be a new program of additional federal funds. The appropriations committees disliked being bypassed by an authorization drawing directly on the treasury, but their complaints proved futile. The main committee concern was one of principle, not program: Wilbur Mills, some other members of the Ways and Means Committee, and (to a lesser degree) members of the Senate Finance Committee questioned the wisdom of allocating sizable sums of federal money to state and local governments without federal conditions. This concern was overcome by a formidable exercise of interest group activity: the intergovernmental lobby of state and local officials, enticed by a $5 billion answer to their fiscal woes, put heavy pressure on Mills and his colleagues to rethink their principles. These were the only lobbies of major importance in the legislative struggle, which was, in Beer's term, a case of "public sector politics." Finally, the absence of categoricals to be consolidated at the state level meant that although the state share of the new revenue-sharing funds was an issue, new state control over old programs was not.

COMMUNITY DEVELOPMENT

The unsuccessful administration proposals to devolve rural development, education, and (to a lesser degree) law enforcement programs struck at the heart of their congressional committees' jurisdictions. By contrast, the programs that would form the community development block grant— urban renewal, model cities, and five other small programs—were relatively minor components of the workload of the subcommittees of the House and Senate Banking and Currency committees that considered them. These were housing subcommittees, and the big, controversial subsidized housing programs, their main concern, lay beyond the scope of the administration's special revenue-sharing packages. Five of the programs to be merged— basic water and sewer facilities, the combined open space–urban beautification–historic preservation programs (consolidated in 1970), neighborhood facilities, rehabilitation loans, and advance acquisition of land—had small budgets and little visibility. Urban renewal and model cities were weightier, but renewal had become controversial since its enactment in 1949, and model cities was new, limited to 150 cities, and already highly devolved, a "mayor's program" by design. Neither renewal nor model cities were highly popular tried and proven solutions to the problems of urban America, or in need of protection and enlargement, as the rural development and education programs were generally thought to be by their respective constituencies.

The community development programs were almost wholly public-sector programs, under the control of local officials all along. No major national private lobbies or public employee organizations were deeply involved in their fate. Whereas the homebuilders, the bankers, and many other private groups rallied to defend their interests in discussions of changes in the subsidized housing programs, the community development programs were of interest mainly to the National League of Cities and U.S. Conference of Mayors, the National Association of Counties, and the National Association of Housing and Redevelopment Officials. All agreed on principles: the "no-strings revenue sharing" proposed by the administration would not do, but consolidation of programs into block grants preserving reasonable federal supervision, as proposed by the subcommittees, was desirable. The groups' arguments addressed matters of detail and were predictable. The local executives wanted changes in the funding formula, revisions in the hold-harmless provisions that protected them from sudden decreases in federal aid, as small a matching share as possible, a fairer shake for small cities, and the exclusion of model cities—a "social" program said to be ill-suited for consolidation with hardware programs—from the block grant.[73] The counties wanted to increase their own opportunities to receive the block grant. The renewal officials hoped that the consolidated grant would secure the status of renewal programs and agencies, which had come under sharp attack from several quarters. Other groups, often strongly protective of individual programs in other policy areas, joined the consensus. For example, both the AFL-CIO and the Urban League agreed that the administration's plan was flawed but that the congressional plan for consolidation in a block grant was satisfactory.[74] An occasional dissent was heard: the National Association of Homebuilders, for example, challenged the block grant concept and argued for retaining the identity of the rehabilitation loan program. But on the whole it is fair

73. *Housing and Urban Development Legislation–1971*, Hearings before the Subcommittee on Housing of the House Committee on Banking and Currency, 92 Cong. 1 sess. (GPO, 1971), pp. 501–06.
74. Ibid., pp. 495–96, 690–96.

to say that community development block grants encountered no extensive organized opposition.

Powerful private interests did not oppose the block grant because they had no major stake in the programs to be consolidated. The public lobbies did not oppose it because community development devolution, unlike that considered in the failed cases, raised no threat of a state takeover. Indeed it is questionable whether this program consolidation should be called "devolution" at all: federal strings were loosened in programs where they had never been very tight, and seven programs were consolidated into one, but there occurred no shift *among* levels of government. Until 1973, "neither the prior administration bill nor the Senate and House bills . . . included any role for State governments except as potential recipients of secretarial discretionary funds." In 1973 the administration proposed "a significant but limited State role,"[75] but there was never any doubt that the state role in the program would be very minor at best. Community development was thus spared the protracted battles between local governments and states and between specialized bureaucracies and governors that helped defeat devolution in the fields of rural development, education, and law enforcement.

When the administration proposed its special revenue-sharing bill in 1971, the committees were already at work on consolidation measures of their own. Indeed, the Senate passed an urban block grant in 1972, which died with the omnibus housing act of that year. Committees could have written and worked for alternatives to the administration's proposals in "failed" fields too; that they did not bother to do so is an excellent measure of their satisfaction with the categorical system (and of their skepticism about the LEAA block grant). In sum, the community development categoricals engaged few congressional protectors, private interests were little involved, public interests were united in support of consolidation, and no divisive issues of state control arose. For these reasons, agreement was reached easily and early that consolidation by means of block grants was desirable. Enactment was then delayed by controversy about the subsidized housing programs, which scuttled the omnibus housing bill and triggered Nixon's 1973 freeze on new commitments.

By the end of 1973 the local officials were desperate. On behalf of the

75. *Housing and Community Development Legislation–1973*, Hearings before the Subcommittee on Housing of the House Committee on Banking and Currency, 93 Cong. 1 sess. (GPO, 1973), p. 308.

League of Cities and Conference of Mayors, the mayor of Trenton complained that the Nixon administration was phasing out the community development categoricals by means of "various shortfunding decisions, terminations, and impoundments." He warned that if Congress did not act quickly, the programs would "shut down altogether by the end of the current fiscal year."[76] The position of the model cities program was an indicator of their anxiety. In 1971 the mayors' lobby had urged that it be excluded from the consolidation, but in 1973 the president of the National Model Cities Community Development Directors Association urged that the program be included.[77] The spokesmen clearly preferred that the program be merged and allowed to fight for life at the local level rather than be retained as a separate program at the tender mercies of the Nixon administration.

MANPOWER

In essentials, manpower politics resembled those of the community development program. Since enactment of the Manpower Development and Training Act of 1962, manpower programs had proliferated, and virtually everyone agreed that the system was needlessly complex and fragmented. As Kenneth Gibson, mayor of Newark, observed, the committees had "heard volumes of testimony over nearly a decade" on the need for better coordination of manpower programs.[78] There were more than 10,000 different contracts between the Department of Labor and local program sponsors, and the mayor of San Jose complained that his relatively small city had fifty to sixty different programs under eighteen prime sponsors.[79] The community action programs (CAPs), whose reputation had been badly tarnished by the early 1970s, sponsored many of these fragmented efforts. Virtually everyone agreed that a one-stop contact point for manpower programs would benefit trainees. This in turn implied a single prime sponsor, and this could hardly be other than each city's mayor. There was broad agreement on the need for consolidation. In this case too the committees—the Select Subcommittee on Labor of the House Education and

76. Ibid., p. 373.

77. Ibid., pp. 436–46.

78. *Comprehensive Manpower Reform–1972*, Hearings before the Subcommittee on Employment, Manpower, and Poverty of the Senate Committee on Labor and Public Welfare, 92 Cong. 2 sess. (GPO, 1972), p. 383.

79. *Comprehensive Manpower Act of 1973*, H. Rept. 659, 93 Cong. 1 sess., p. 2; and *Comprehensive Manpower Reform–1972*, Hearings, p. 491.

Labor Committee, and the Subcommittee on Employment, Manpower, and Poverty of the Senate Labor and Public Welfare Committee—quickly devised their own measures in competition with the administration's special revenue-sharing plan.

Furthermore, the manpower programs had much the same ancillary relation to the labor subcommittees' primary concern—public service employment—that the community development programs had in relation to the housing subcommittees' primary concern—subsidized housing. Most committee members appeared to agree with the AFL-CIO that "the key to effective manpower policy is job creation."[80] Consolidating manpower training programs was an important but secondary item on the committees' agendas, and a bargaining chip as Congress sought the administration's acquiescence in creating a large public jobs program.

The agencies that ran the manpower programs and the constituencies that benefited from them were no more willing to fight consolidation than were those in the community development field. Programs in both areas were increasingly vulnerable to the Nixon administration's aggressive unilateral impoundments, cutbacks, and reorganizations. Even as the mayors feared that the end was drawing near for community development programs starved by the fund freeze of 1973, the community action program narrowly escaped destruction by the administration, whose attempt to shut down the agency was declared illegal in court. Their role as prime sponsors would be removed, to be sure, but the CAPs, like the model cities agencies, preferred to take their chances locally under new block grant legislation rather than watch their activities (and perhaps their existence) ended by executive fiat.

Community development devolution was an almost pure case of public-sector politics, fought out mainly between mayors and county officials. Public-sector politics was the core of CETA politics too. The most influential groups were again the National League of Cities, the U.S. Conference of Mayors, and the National Association of Counties. Control over job training and hiring was a political prize denied the local politicians by direct Labor Department contracts with community groups. Awareness of this deprivation no doubt explains the "volumes of testimony over nearly a decade" of protest. Interest group politics in CETA differed from those in the CDBG in two important ways, however. First, prodded by the administration's

80. *Job Training and Employment Legislation, 1973,* Hearings before the Subcommittee on Employment, Poverty, and Migratory Labor of the Senate Committee on Labor and Public Welfare, 93 Cong. 1 sess. (GPO, 1973), p. 494.

special revenue-sharing approach, the states (meaning in this case the governors and state employment services), who obviously could hope for no important role in the CDBG, sought to expand their roles in the manpower block grant program. The second exception, however, largely explains why the mayors and counties prevailed in CETA as they also did in the CDBG: the AFL-CIO, a private-sector interest group of fundamental importance in manpower politics (and with no clear analogue in the CDBG), strongly supported the mayors and counties in preference to the governors.

The policy consensus that supported one-stop contact points, fewer prime sponsors, and coordination under the authority of public officials also maintained that the identity of prime sponsors should be reasonably related to the scope of local or regional labor markets. In most cases, local or county government, not the states, met this criterion. Moreover, the state employment services were thought by many to be "falling down on the job" in their efforts to train the disadvantaged.[81] Despite the efforts of the governors, the employment services, and the administration to enlarge the state role, the solid coalition of mayors, counties, and organized labor coming before urban-oriented, liberal committees ensured that the states had no chance to prevail. As an outcome drew near in 1973, a spokesman for the governors noted that when the manpower debate began in 1969, the states had argued for "a near dominant role" in manpower programs. Since then they had made "tremendous concessions," reconciling themselves to the prospect that cities and counties with populations of 100,000 or 150,000 would be directly funded.[82] Vocational education, a popular, well-connected program of ancient vintage (1917) won special status in the law (as did the Job Corps), and the manpower block grant, like that for community development, did much more consolidating than devolving: local programs were combined at the local level, the states left largely on the sidelines.

The Irony of Structural Politics

The structural politics of the devolution successes were both highly contingent and ironic. In some versions of federalist theory, orderly de-

---

81. The Lawyers' Committee for Civil Rights under Law and the National Urban Coalition, "Falling Down on the Job: The United States Employment Service and the Disadvantaged," June 1971; reprinted in *Comprehensive Manpower Reform—1972*, Hearings, pp. 1273–1406.

82. *Comprehensive Manpower Act of 1973*, Hearings before the Select Subcommittee on Labor of the House Committee on Education and Labor, 93 Cong. 1 sess. (GPO, 1974), p. 110.

volution in a federal system relies heavily on the states as intermediary between the central and local governments. A key to the enactment of the community development and manpower block grants, however, was elimination of the threat of state control and the triumph of local and county executives. These executives, in turn, were able to prevail mainly because they were the only (or the major) interest groups at work—they had the policy domain to themselves because (1) the programs at issue were mainly specimens of public-sector politics, created by reformers in and out of government at government's invitation, with few private-sector constituencies to defend them; and (2) the committees considering consolidation were receptive. The committees, in turn, were receptive mainly because the programs were secondary items on their agenda, no longer offered ready opportunities for claiming political credit, and had come under sharp attack in the crisis of urban liberalism.

Nixon's determination to batter the "establishment" of agencies, groups, and committees by means of devolution also succumbed to irony: the establishment held fast where it was most established, yielding only where it had been weak all along. In the success cases, programs that had always been heavily local were made more so, interest groups were less protective of their programs, and congressmen were only weakly committed to them. In programs where there *was* an establishment worthy of the name— where congressional committee members remained loyal to and convinced of the worth of categorical programs (or were skeptical of block grants); interest groups were numerous, private, well-organized, or closely identified with their programs; and there was a genuine threat that generalist state politicians would replace functional specialists in running programs— devolution was rejected.

Strategy: Successes and Failures

In the four cases of failure, the combined force of inhospitable values and structures precluded any strategy of building a coalition in support of devolution. In the three successful cases, several conditions—executive determination, a climate of opinion in which categoricals were found wanting, receptive legislative committee leadership, and weak institutionalization of opposing interests—set the stage for coalition-building strategies with a serious chance of success. The favorable interplay of value and structure created merely the *chance* of change, however; enactment of legislation required strategic adroitness and compromise in finding terms that both the Republican executive and a majority of both houses of a Democratic legislature could endorse.

Four Success Strategies

In the three success cases, coalition building consisted of four basic strategic steps. First, the monetary stakes were expanded. Much to the chagrin of fiscal conservatives, who had viewed revenue sharing as a means of curbing or reversing the growth of federal spending, Nixon did not long hesitate to increase massively his proposed authorizations for general revenue sharing in order to awaken the interest of the intergovernmental lobby. The lobby, which had yawned at the $1 billion proposed in 1969, sprang into action at the mention of $5 billion in 1971. The strategy, Nathan and Calkins remark, was to inflate the funding and then to dangle printouts before the eyes of eligible jurisdictions' officials to stimulate interest and political support.[83] The strategy worked very well: by 1972 Wilbur Mills, who had earlier promised to kill general revenue sharing, had become a proponent, and Congress, happy to join the expansionist game, ended by appropriating an annual average sum of over $6 billion for the program.

In the special revenue-sharing proposals, the administration combined sticks—threats of impoundments, freezes, spending delays, and vetoes of appropriation bills—with carrots—the promise that devolved packages would enjoy the sum of existing categorical appropriations plus a modest sweetener. In the failure cases, the threats were either politically risky for the administration or dispelled by indignant legislators and strong interest groups, and the modest sweeteners were greeted contemptuously by lawmakers and groups, who viewed them as insensitive to problems requiring large new federal commitments. In the community development and manpower programs, however, the threats had already been carried out and the sweeteners looked very inviting when the alternative was recurrent rounds of vetoes, impoundments, and freezes. In 1975 the $2.8 billion Congress appropriated for community development granted the president's full request and raised it by about $50 million; the $3.3 billion appropriation the following year was about $87 million above the administration's request. For the manpower programs Congress passed a supplemental appropriation in May 1974 of $2.26 billion, almost $500 million above the president's request.

83. "The Story of Revenue Sharing." p. 26.

A second strategy was the expansion of eligible jurisdictions. As noted above, local fear of an expanded state role was a major factor in the failures, and the successes were realized only after the threat of state preeminence had been eliminated. The states could not be entirely excluded from devolved programs, however, and the universe of localities itself contained several jealous factions: counties and suburbs sought to increase their standing alongside the cities, and the interests of larger cities often differed from those of small cities, townships, and villages.

A share of program funds large enough to win the political support of one of these factions might also be large enough to alienate the others. The only practical solution was simultaneously to increase the dollar authorizations and expand the definition of eligible jurisdictions. In the general revenue-sharing program, one-third of the funds went to the states, two-thirds to localities. Proponents of administrative rationality might carp all they pleased about the minimum size of an efficient local government unit, but general revenue sharing rejected a proposed cutoff at localities of 2,500 residents and extended eligibility to virtually all government units in the United States.

In the course of shrinking thousands of manpower contracts between the Department of Labor and local community organizations to a few hundred between Labor and governmental prime sponsors, CETA extended prime sponsorship to any "unit of general local government" with a population of more than 100,000. The counties fought hard and successfully for inclusion, and in fiscal year 1975 there were 403 eligible prime sponsors, 156 of them counties, 134 consortia of governmental units. Most of these prime sponsors had not received federal manpower funds before.[84]

The community development legislation not only contained a hold harmless provision that protected recipients of categorical aid against decreases for five years but also greatly expanded eligible jurisdictions, about one-third of which had received few or no categorical community development monies before. In the CDBG as in CETA, this inclusiveness was largely the result of aggressive lobbying by the National Association of Counties, determined not to leave the field to its brethren in the National League of Cities and U.S. Conference of Mayors.[85]

84. Advisory Commission on Intergovernmental Relations, *The Comprehensive Employment and Training Act: Early Readings from a Hybrid Block Grant*, A-58 (ACIR, June 1977), pp. 23–24.

85. Paul R. Dommel and associates, *Decentralizing Urban Policy: Case Studies in Community Development* (Brookings Institution, 1982), pp. 35–36.

A third strategy was to manipulate formulas to achieve diffusion of funds *among* these very broadly defined eligible jurisdictions. Beer has shown how coalition building for general revenue sharing steered resolutely between the two "logical" allocative principles of need and merit and ended up with a formula that honored neither, embracing instead a rule of approximately equal per capita distribution.[86] Diffusion of funding in the community development program made winners of the suburbs and losers of the central cities, which had received 72 percent of the categorical budget and now received only 42 percent of the block grant.[87] In CETA too, "the principal effect of the distribution formula [was] to shift dollars from cities to counties."[88]

Fourth, devolution proponents expanded their coalitions by eliminating controversial strings imposed on the recipients of federal aid. In the debates about the three success cases, skeptics sometimes questioned whether it was wise for the federal government to hand out large sums to a long list of jursidictions of uneven capacities and intentions without some accompanying legislative definition of sound practices and procedures. Such definitions, however, threatened to weaken the coalitions, and many were eliminated or softened.

For example, when the House included "priority-expenditure categories" in its version of the general revenue-sharing bill, the Senate balked. The conference committee "expanded the House list substantially and permitted all types of capital expenditures. The net result was to dilute significantly the effect of the priority categories."[89] The conferees refused to impose maintenance-of-effort requirements on recipients. Michael Reagan summed up the strategy by noting that program recipients reported their use of funds "in a standardized format, but with no directions whatsoever as to where the emphasis in expenditures shall be placed, with the one exception that they are not permitted to spend revenue sharing funds on school operation and maintenance." This, he remarks, "is the only programmatic 'string' attached to general revenue sharing."[90]

The community development title required that recipient localities draw

86. "The Adoption of General Revenue Sharing," pp. 147–49.

87. Dommel, *Decentralizing Urban Policy*, p. 41.

88. ACIR, *The Comprehensive Employment and Training Act*, p. 37.

89. Richard P. Nathan and others, *Monitoring Revenue Sharing* (Brookings Institution, 1975), p. 371.

90. Michael D. Reagan, "Revenue Sharing: The Pro and Con Arguments," in Alan Shank, ed., *American Politics, Policies, and Priorities*, 3d ed. (Allyn and Bacon, 1981), p. 127.

up plans describing how they would eliminate or prevent slums, blight, and deterioration; allowed HUD to veto unacceptable applications; and instructed localities to give local residents a chance to participate in devising applications and plans. The law was vague and unspecific, however, about the contents of such plans, the means to be employed, the structure and organization of the local program, and the nature and scope of resident participation.[91]

Provisions in CETA emphasized targeting, coordination, and planning, but these provisions too were for the most part generally worded and vague. For example, the Labor Department was told to approve prime sponsors' plans only if they showed that manpower services would "to the maximum extent feasible" be provided to those "most in need," but, except for "including low-income persons and persons of limited English-speaking ability," the law declined to be explicit. Likewise, it required that "continued funding of programs of demonstrated effectiveness" be "taken into account," but it did not name the programs.[92] In writing these provisions, Congress was faithful to the understanding of devolution it had maintained all along: block grants were distinct from both the no-strings special revenue-sharing approach of the administration and from the string-encumbered categorical approach of the past.

Each of these four strategies departed sharply from the principles of allocation according to need and merit, principles that had been honored, at least in theory, in the categorical grant-in-aid system. The outcome— extreme diffusion of sizable sums of federal aid among and within localities, with relatively little federal influence on the uses of the aid—was an equally sharp departure, but one that was unavoidable once the politics of coalition building were set in motion.

Why the Strategies Succeeded

The success of these strategies is largely explained by three factors. First, Nixon's faith in decentralization (or better, defederalization) for its own sake made him indifferent to the financial and normative costs of the sticks and carrots required to build a coalition for his proposals. Second, disillusionment and political embarrassment inhibited liberals who had defended the categories of need and merit in the past. Third, the context

91. Dommel, *Decentralizing Urban Policy*, pp. 28–32.
92. 87 Stat. 844.

of legislative-executive bargaining encouraged the quest for quid pro quos. In general revenue sharing, the executive wanted legislative votes and needed the intergovernmental lobby to get them; the strategies described above were fine-tuned until they met this need. In the manpower field, the executive wanted reorganization and consolidation, while important parts of Congress wanted public service employment. CETA was part of the bargain struck. In the community development field, the executive sought consolidation, while Congress wanted funds for the frozen categorical programs to flow again. The community development block grants achieved both objectives.

In these cases as always, the structure of legislative-executive relations made bargaining necessary. But in these three cases, unlike many others, the climate of opinion made bargaining attractive, the structure of public and private interests made it promising, and the specific strategies of inclusion and diffusion made it succeed. Neither values, structures, nor strategies offered comparable bargaining opportunities in the cases of failure.

The Unstable Politics of Devolution in the Post-Nixon Years

The devolution triumphs of 1972–74 were limited, circumstantial innovations, not first, decisive steps down the road to comprehensive reform of the grant-in-aid system, nor emblems of a basic shift in the politics of American federalism. Enactment of general revenue sharing depended heavily on the coincidence of the fiscal crisis of the states and localities and the political crisis of Great Society liberalism. The block grant successes depended importantly on the peculiar political properties of the manpower and urban development policy arenas. In policy arenas where these peculiarities and coincidences were not found, the categorical approach remained alive and well.

The Ford and Carter Administrations

Between 1974 and 1981 the politics of devolution came to a near halt. The legislation establishing the CDBG, the third and last of Nixon's triumphs, was signed by Gerald Ford shortly after Nixon left office in disgrace. In 1976 Ford proposed new block grants for health, education, child nutrition, and social services, but Congress declined to act on them.[93] In 1976 Congress created new public jobs in title VI of CETA over Ford's objection (it had passed in 1974 with his support) and authorized new programs of public works and countercyclical aid over his veto. Early in the Carter administration these programs were expanded to an economic stimulus package of more than $15 billion, of which about $3 billion was revenue-sharing funds for cities with higher-than-average unemployment. These efforts triggered jurisdictional jealousies and concerns about the widening federal deficit, however, and despite predictions that Congress would find it impossible to end a package so large and so important to the cities, countercyclical aid was allowed to expire at the end of September 1978. This was Carter's sole venture in revenue sharing; although he had much to say about improving and simplifying the operations of the federal government, he showed little inclination to transfer its power to subnational units.

As the 1970s wore on, the devolved programs were evaluated in light of accumulating experience. The early block grant programs received low grades for both effectiveness and efficiency. The partnership for health program of 1966 languished in political limbo for several years. In 1974 the comprehensive health planning agencies it had created were converted into supposedly stronger health systems agencies. By 1980 these too had fallen into disfavor and the Reagan administration targeted them for extinction. (As of 1984, however, Congress was still keeping some of them alive.) The accomplishments of the model cities program, also created in 1966, were widely judged to be few and small, one major reason being that the cities in the program were often not organized to spend the money sensibly.[94] The LEAA, enacted in 1968 and reauthorized in 1973, continued to suffer from managerial and other difficulties. Extended again in 1976 with diminished funds, the program was permitted to expire unmourned in 1980. Early predictions that LEAA grants supporting "more of the same" at the local level would achieve little have apparently been confirmed.[95]

93. The title XX program of social services grants cleared by Congress in December 1974 was dubbed a block grant but it consolidated no programs. Instead, it capped federal spending for these grants and in exchange gave the states greater discretion in their use. See Martha Derthick, *Uncontrollable Spending for Social Service Grants* (Brookings Institution, 1975).

94. Lawrence D. Brown, "Coordination of Federal Urban Policy: Organizational Politics in Three Model Cities" (Ph.D. dissertation, Harvard University, 1973).

95. For example, James Q. Wilson, *Thinking about Crime* (Basic Books, 1975), p. 208: "Nearly ten years ago I wrote that the billions of dollars the federal government was then preparing to spend on crime control would be wasted, and indeed might even make matters worse if they were merely pumped into the existing criminal justice system. They were, and they have."

The Nixonian triumphs have also traveled a rocky road. In the 1970s state and local finances improved while the federal budget deficit worsened. As popular pressure for a balanced federal budget grew, politicians began wondering aloud whether it made sense to increase the federal budget shortfall merely to enlarge the surpluses of states and well-off localities. Signs of stress were evident when the general revenue-sharing program came up for extension in 1976. President Ford wanted the program reauthorized for more than five years at more than $40 billion, with built-in annual increases. Congress agreed only to an extension of three years and nine months at $25 billion. This figure preserved the then-current annual average—$6.65 billion—and Congress refused to continue the automatic annual increases of the original program.

By 1980 federal revenue-sharing funds for the states had become controversial. After much debate, the program was extended, but the state share for fiscal year 1981 was eliminated. Until the Reagan administration took office, the local share was secure, but that administration began to question whether revenue sharing was compatible with the principles of its own New Federalism. That the program has continued may be testimony to the power of the intergovernmental lobby. On the other hand, the growing fragility of the federal government's biggest giveaway program— a program, in Beer's term, of "breathtaking promiscuity," giving large string-free sums to each state and to virtually every unit of local government[96]— may suggest that the lobby's power to sustain an outcome based on little more than logrolling and unsupported by arguments based on traditional principles of need and merit may be weakening.[97]

The manpower block grant has been controversial too. Soon after CETA got under way, complaints arose that funds were being used for worthless projects, to support routine local expenses, and to rehire laid-off public employees; that the program was doing much less than expected to train the poor and disadvantaged; and that some cities were spending money dishonestly. Many of these criticisms applied more to the public employment titles than to the block grant, but in some eyes both were tarred with the same brush. When the Carter administration addressed these complaints by tightening administrative restrictions on the use of CETA monies, local officials complained of "recategorization" and began to lose interest

96. Beer, "The Adoption of General Revenue Sharing," p. 148; and Nathan and Calkins, "The Story of Revenue Sharing," p. 34.

97. For a discussion of some problems in the program see Dommel, *Politics of Revenue Sharing*, pp. 175–94.

in the program. A 1978 reauthorization of CETA redesigned eligibility to favor the long-term over the recently unemployed. In 1981 Congress agreed to the Reagan administration's request that public service employment funds be eliminated and those for other titles be cut severely; protests were surprisingly mild and ineffective.

The community development block grant program has achieved relative stability and acceptance, perhaps because it was the least ambitious of the three successes: in essence the CDBG merged two big programs, one old and faded (renewal), the other young and faded (model cities), and surrounded them with five very small and uncontroversial programs amounting in total to only 10 percent of the block grant funds. Nonetheless questions about the equity of urban aid have been directed at the CDBG too. From the beginning, organizations representing the poor charged that many cities defined "community development" so as to emphasize projects of interest to the middle class, such as wrapping up long-lingering urban renewal projects.[98] Academic proponents of targeting argued that the formula adopted in 1974 spread money too widely, concentrating too little on hardship sites.[99] In 1977 the critics won a revision in the formula to include the percentage of housing built before 1940, a good proxy for conditions of old, poor central cities. Although this change produced a greater degree of targeting, the effect was modest.[100] Critics have continued to press the case for targeting in the language of the traditional values of the categorical approach: why should so much federal money be devoted to cities and suburbs that do not need it, while relatively small sums go to those with grave problems? But now that the values that braked promiscuous localism have been so thoroughly compromised, little can be done. The new legions of local voluptuaries will not consent to the redistribution required to target, and sweetening by increasing the size of the pot for all is no longer feasible.

The Reagan Administration

In 1980 the election of Ronald Reagan brought the devolution strategy to life again. On taking office Reagan announced his commitment to yet

98. Cole's data, however, suggest that "most of the funds are being spent in low-income areas of the recipient communities." "The Politics of Housing and Community Development in America," pp. 115–21, quotation at p. 121.

99. Ibid., pp. 118, 124; and Dommel, *Decentralizing Urban Policy*, pp. 34–43.

100. Dommel, *Decentralizing Urban Policy*, pp. 253–55.

another New Federalism, this one based on decentralization (block grants to the states) and substitution (deep federal budget cuts that did not spare the programs to be devolved). Like Nixon, Reagan won enactment of some of his program, but in a much revised and reduced form. The trio of variables employed here helps explain these recent politics of devolution.

VALUES

Devolution politics in 1981 reflected a resurgence of decentralist ideology. Reagan's anticentralist campaign attacked all the works and ways of the federal government and blamed it for virtually all of society's ills. (Indeed, if one were to take Reagan's reading of American history literally, one might conclude that the federal government was little more than an afterthought invented for the convenience of the separate states.) Reagan's victory was hardly a popular landslide (he carried about 51 percent of the vote), and it may have demonstrated disdain for the competence of the Carter administration more than for the federal government itself. However, the circumstances of the victory—Reagan carried forty-four states, threw an elected incumbent president out of office for the first time since 1932, and helped elect the first Republican Senate since 1952—naturally gave it the aura of a decentralist mandate. Democrats were embarrassed by Carter's rejection, by their new minority status in the Senate, by the narrowing of their majority in the House, and by the unmistakable (though perhaps temporary) infatuation of the electorate with right-wing ideology. The crisis of urban liberalism of the early 1970s had by 1981 grown into a crisis of liberalism itself. In 1981 a Republican executive zealous for decentralization again confronted a dispirited liberal opposition reluctant to defend the preservation of federal power in the grant-in-aid system.

STRUCTURE

The Republican executive seeking devolution in 1981 enjoyed a Republican Senate, an advantage his counterpart in the early 1970s never had. The structural contrast is instructive. In 1972 Nixon won reelection by a landslide against a Democratic opponent thought to be out of touch with the national mood. He returned to Washington with a sense of vindication, a mandate, and an agenda for change, including a hit list of federal programs to be ended, and new proposals for special revenue sharing in the New Federalism. He played very roughly indeed, but despite impoundments, vetoes, freezes, delayed outlays, and an illegal effort to shut down the Office of Economic Opportunity, in the end he eliminated next to nothing and won enactment of only two block grants. The influence of Watergate is difficult to assess, but unquestionably the solidly Democratic Congress gave political weight to opponents of devolution both inside and outside it, and thereby confined legislative successes to especially vulnerable areas. The existence of three power centers—president, House, and Senate—generally gives legislative-executive politics the character of a game in which "best two out of three" wins. Assuming unity within a Republican-controlled Senate, a Democrat-controlled House will be in a weak position to block the agenda of a popular Republican president.

This change in public power structure at the federal level changed in turn the role of the private and public power structures in devolution debates. Put simply, the Republican Senate meant that Reagan did not need the intergovernmental lobby in his quest for new block grants. Facing two Democratic chambers with deep reservations about devolution, Nixon needed political allies. In practice they could only be interest groups with a tangible stake in devolution, and these would offer support only if the money stakes were raised sufficiently that they found it worth their while to exert themselves on behalf of a political figure they tended to distrust. Political reality forced Nixon to couple decentralization with supplementation, promising large new sums (general revenue sharing), accepting a new program along with devolution of old programs (CETA), and restoring the flow of frozen funds in still others (CDBG).

The 1980 election changed decisively both the structure and the content of devolution politics. Enjoying a "mandate," a Republican Senate, and a more conservative (albeit Democratic) House, Reagan could wed decentralization to substitution, cutting strings and funds simultaneously. The intergovernmental lobby obligingly offered to accept funding cuts of 10 percent in exchange for reduced federal strings on grants-in-aid. Reagan proposed, and Congress accepted, cuts of about 25 percent along with reductions in federal constraints. Having won these cuts, Reagan proposed a 12 percent reduction in the general revenue-sharing program. Eager to learn of the administration's plans for returning federal revenues to them, state and local officials heard a Treasury official explain that federal tax cuts gave the subnational governments "extra taxing room," and that the federal government could do little more for them. The Treasury official was skeptical of revenue sharing: in perhaps the most ironic utterance in the history of devolution politics, he proclaimed that "true federalism" demanded that the same unit of government that collects the taxes should spend the money, and added that "any form of revenue sharing—whatever form it takes—interferes with the efficiency and rationality of decisions made when the same unit does the taxing and spending." The state and local officials greeted these declarations with "expressions of astonishment and protest."[101]

STRATEGY

The combined force of values and structure put Reagan in the strongest political position a devolution proponent has yet enjoyed. Congressional action on his block grant proposals is therefore a good indicator of the degree to which devolution had gained strength since the Nixon victories. The most important Reagan proposals called for consolidation of twenty-five health programs into two block grants, forty-four education programs into two block grants, and thirteen social services programs into one grant and a modest consolidation of a handful of energy assistance programs.[102] Given his political strength, Reagan won surprisingly little.

The House and Senate responded to the energy block grant proposal by retaining the existing low-income energy assistance program, but calling it a block grant. They declined to merge a welfare-related energy assistance program with it, but they did reduce federal controls.

Social services block grants met with little enthusiasm in the House, and the Senate, which acted on the proposal, altered it considerably, retaining several categoricals. Ultimately, the new "block grant" simply merged title XX, an existing block grant, with a categorical social services training program, leaving out all the other categoricals on the administration's list.

Education block grants met opposition in the House and from education

---

101. *The Washington Post*, October 23, 1981.

102. The account given here of Reagan's proposals and their congressional reception draws on *Congressional Quarterly Almanac*, vol. 37 (1981), pp. 463–64, 484–85, 499 (the numbers of programs and block grants cited in the text come from this source); Rochelle L. Stanfield, "Block Grants Look Fine to States; It's the Money That's the Problem," *National Journal*, vol. 13 (May 9, 1981), pp. 828–32; "Congress Works a Minor Revolution—Making Cuts to Meet Its Budget Goals," *National Journal*, vol. 13 (June 20, 1981), pp. 1114–25, especially pp. 1115, 1118; Richard E. Cohen, "For Spending Cuts, Only the Beginning," *National Journal*, vol. 13 (August 8, 1981), p. 1414; *Congressional Quarterly Weekly Reports*, vol. 39 (May 23, 1981), pp. 907–08; June 6, 1981, pp. 1005–08; June 20, 1981, pp. 1080–87; July 4, 1981, pp. 1180–82; July 25, 1981, pp. 1328–30; August 1, 1981, pp. 1387–90; and David B. Walker and others, "The First Ten Months: Grant-in-Aid, Regulatory, and Other Changes," *Intergovernmental Perspective*, vol. 8 (Winter 1982), pp. 5–22, especially pp. 8–9, 12. It should also be noted that the administration won enactment of an "entitlement areas" block grant, a spinoff of CDBG, and a community services block grant that consolidated several categoricals.

interest groups, and found only very guarded acceptance in the Senate. Robert Stafford, Republican of Vermont, new chairman of the education subcommittee of the Senate Labor and Human Resources Committee, observed that the ESEA existed because the states had failed to aid the disadvantaged;[103] it was clear from the start that Reagan's proposal would not pass intact. Stafford's subcommittee hit upon a simple solution: exclude the large, strongly supported programs for the disadvantaged, handicapped, migrants and others, and fashion a block grant from various small, weakly supported programs.[104] The House accepted this compromise. In the end Reagan won enactment not of two block grants comprising more than $4 billion of education programs, but of one, a modest measure of about $589 million.

The health block grant proposals encountered immediate resistance not only from House Democrats, but also from two Republican members of the Senate Labor and Human Resources Committee (Stafford and Lowell Weicker of Connecticut), who joined seven Democrats to outvote their seven Republican colleagues. After long debate and bitter negotiations, conferees agreed on four block grants. One, primary care, was a new name for the community health center program, which the states would now run. The second contained seven maternal and child health programs, but retained a state matching requirement and imposed several restrictions on the use of funds. A third combined three programs aimed at alcoholism, drug abuse, and mental health, but required that states spend 35 percent of their substance abuse funds on alcohol treatment, and 35 percent on drug abuse, leaving 30 percent to state discretion. The fourth, the preventive health and health services grant, consolidated eight relatively obscure programs—rat control, fluoridation, education to reduce health risks, and so on—but earmarked funds for two of the more popular, rape crisis centers and hypertension control. Several programs—among them family planning, venereal disease control, and migrant health centers—remained categorical. Ironically, the compromise that preserved the family planning program created perhaps the most widely noticed new categorical: federal funds to establish a network of local centers to persuade teenagers of the virtues of chastity.

103. *Congressional Quarterly Weekly Reports*, vol. 39 (June 6, 1981), p. 1008.

104. One of these was the tiny metric education program, whose creator and protector, Senator Claiborne Pell, Democrat of Rhode Island, lost power when the Senate went Republican. See the vignette of this program in Rochelle L. Stanfield, "Bureaucrat Can't Count on His Old Allies," *National Journal*, vol. 13 (March 28, 1981), pp. 525–27.

When the dust had settled, the categorical grant-in-aid system had survived in reasonably good health the most resolute attack on it to date by the most powerful political antagonist it had yet encountered. Some consolidation of small health and education programs had been accomplished, but the energy block grant was a semantic invention, most of the social services grant lay in shreds on the conference room floor, the education grant had shrunk from a $4 billion fantasy to a $0.6 billion reality, and many parts of the four health grants were hemmed in with exclusions, earmarkings, and mandates. The Republican unity that held so firmly in defense of the Reagan budget cuts cracked in the crucial committee stages on the issue of devolution.

Under intense pressure to cut both program budgets and categorical ties between the federal and subnational governments, Congress proved far readier to do the former than the latter. As Richard Nathan pointed out, a projected decline of 15 percent in real domestic spending between 1981 and 1985 could be viewed as "a basic shift" in federal spending priorities.[105] On the other hand, Reagan's original proposal for seven block grants amounting to $16.5 billion in federal funds had been transformed by Congress into nine block grants accounting for only $7.5 billion, and only four of these—with a total of $1.5 billion in 1982 budget authority—"might properly be regarded as new and as involving consequential grant consolidations." In view of the various limitations and restrictions attached by Congress, Nathan concluded that for several so-called block grants the name was "attached to legislation that is a far cry from the genuine article," and that "the structural changes enacted in the name of block grants as part of the Reagan domestic program in 1981 are not very significant." Even in the high tide of the Reagan "revolution," traditional sentiments against devolution remained strong: some states and localities would not deal fairly with the disadvantaged; some would not spend the money wisely; purposes important enough to enjoy the authorization and appropriation of federal funds were important enough to remain under that modicum of control the federal government has traditionally asserted.

In sum, devolution successes remain occasional, episodic, and highly contingent. The only safe generalizations appear to be these: Devolution has become an intrinsic part of the Republican agenda. The prospects for devolution are likely to vary directly with the ideological zeal and political

105. Richard P. Nathan, "Clearing Up the Confusion Over Block Grants," *Wall Street Journal*, November 3, 1981.

strength of the Republican party. The nation may anticipate a continuing parade of "new federalisms," searching scrutiny of and skepticism about the categorical programs of the federal government, and new devolution triumphs when time and circumstance prove favorable. No endorsement of devolution is sweeping American political culture, however, and no orderly and principled devolution of federal activities is in prospect.

JAMES W. FOSSETT

The Politics of Dependence: Federal Aid to Big Cities

THE MAJOR BUILDUP of federal grants to cities during the 1970s led many observers of urban affairs to express concern that city governments were becoming dependent on the federal government as a major source of revenue. Noting the increasing size of federal funds relative to locally raised revenue in the budgets of many cities, one observer was moved to argue that cities were in danger of becoming "creatures of the state and wards of the federal government."

Changes during the 1970s in the federal urban aid system were indeed substantial. Largely as a result of the passage of general revenue-sharing and community development block grant programs under the Nixon and Ford administrations and the major expansion of public jobs and public works programs under the Carter administration, federal grants to cities expanded by over 700 percent between 1970 and 1978, or better than twice the rate of growth in the grant system as a whole.

Federal grants reached their peak as a city revenue source in 1978, when they provided funds equivalent to 26 percent of the revenue cities raised on their own and 70 percent of the revenue provided to cities by state governments. While the rate of growth in direct federal grants has declined sharply in recent years, federal dollars remain a substantial revenue source for city governments. In 1982 direct federal grants amounted to approximately $11 billion, the equivalent of 18.4 percent of city-raised revenue.[1]

The author acknowledges helpful comments on earlier versions of this chapter from Richard P. Nathan, research support of a high order from Ann Geraci, and manuscript preparation and editorial help by Kathryn A. Jones and David Aiken.

1. U.S. Bureau of the Census, *City Government Finances in 1981–82* (Government Printing Office, 1983), table 1, p. 7.

There were also noteworthy changes during the seventies in the geographic allocation of federal funds to cities. Under earlier categorical programs such as urban renewal and model cities, federal administrators reviewed applications from local agencies and granted funds to those that ranked high on various criteria. This method tended to concentrate federal funds in larger cities, particularly in the Northeast, whose officials were willing to invest substantial effort in developing applications and lobbying federal agencies to secure their approval.

The new programs of the seventies, by contrast, allocated funds automatically on the basis of formulas to all cities that met simple eligibility criteria. The general revenue-sharing program, for example, distributes funds to all 38,000 units of general-purpose local government in the country. The community development block grant program provides nearly automatic funding to any city recognized as the central city of a standard metropolitan statistical area. Governments do not have to compete for funds with other governments, but rather receive allocations based on characteristics of the city's population, housing stock, or finances. The increased use of formulas has had the effect of spreading funds to smaller cities throughout the country and to larger cities in the South and West, many of which had received little or no money from earlier programs.[2]

These new programs also produced a major change in the types of recipients within cities. Earlier categorical programs made large numbers of grants to special authorities and community organizations. The formula-based programs of the seventies, by contrast, provide federal funds to city governments, which have a substantial amount of discretion in deciding how to spend them. Organizations such as urban renewal authorities and community action agencies that once dealt directly with federal agencies are now compelled to work through city hall to obtain federal support.

There is, in brief, some plausibility to the argument that cities may have become dependent on federal dollars. Substantial amounts of money are being provided to a large number of cities in a form that makes it relatively easy for city officials to either cut local taxes or increase services with no increases in taxes. Further, redirecting federal funds through city hall may

---

2. For descriptions of changes in the geographic allocation of federal urban aid over this period, see Richard P. Nathan and James W. Fossett, "Urban Conditions—The Future of the Federal Role," in 1978 *Proceedings of the Seventy-first Annual Conference on Taxation* (Columbus, Ohio: National Tax Association–Tax Institute of America, 1979); and Richard P. Nathan, "The Outlook for Federal Grants to Cities," in Roy Bahl, ed., *The Fiscal Outlook for Cities* (Syracuse University Press, 1978).

have provided mayors and council members with the opportunity to use federal funds to maintain or broaden their base of political support. If local officials have availed themselves of these opportunities for fiscal or political relief, then many cities may have in fact become dependent on these funds and may stand to lose substantially from aid cutbacks of the magnitude contained in recent administration proposals.

The extent to which cities have, in fact, used federal dollars in ways that have made them financially or politically dependent is, however, far from clear. Because the federal programs enacted during the seventies presented local officials with a considerable amount of discretion in how to use federal dollars, a reasonable assessment of dependence requires some understanding of the uses of federal dollars and the attitudes of state and local officials toward them.

Current Ways of Measuring Dependence

Most attempts to assess the impact of grants on city budgets simply compare the amount of federal aid a city receives with other types of city income, usually taxes or total revenues from the city's own sources. The logic behind this approach is simple: cities that receive large amounts of federal money relative to other local income are more vulnerable to budget disruptions caused by reductions in federal money—and hence are more dependent on that money—than are cities for which federal funds are a less significant revenue source. A number of scholars and government agencies have relied on such calculations to assess the dependence of different cities at different points over the last several years.[3]

Most researchers who have made these calculations have predicted dire consequences from a major reduction in federal grants to cities. Most large cities, according to these calculations, have come to rely, both financially and politically, on these funds either to keep taxes down or to support city services at levels that could not be sustained in the absence of federal funds. Substantial cuts in federal funds would require either massive cuts

3. See, for example, the calculations reported in U.S. Department of the Treasury, "Report on the Impact of the Economic Stimulus Package on 48 Large Urban Governments" (Department of the Treasury, 1978); Advisory Commission on Intergovernmental Relations, *Federal Stabilization Policy: The Role of State and Local Governments* (GPO, 1978); and Astrid Mergit, "Fiscal Dependency of American Cities," *Public Budgeting and Finance*, vol. 1 (1981), pp. 20–30.

in city services or equally sizable increases in city taxes and would produce significant deterioration in the financial condition and credit position of most big cities. In short, American cities are dependent on federal funds and have been for some time.[4]

The major argument of this essay is that this sort of calculation overstates the financial and political importance of federal funds to most cities and hence the potential consequences of a major reduction in that aid. Although some cities have come to rely quite heavily on federal funds, there are fewer such cities than is commonly believed.

Redefining Dependence

Figures comparing the amount of federal money cities receive with their locally generated revenue can be useful indicators of trends in the distribution of federal funds and the relative size of federal dollars in local budgets. They need to be carefully interpreted, however, because several factors can produce substantial variations in either local or federal revenues, but have little connection to city dependence on federal funds. The following five factors are particularly important.

1. Support from the state or other overlying governments. Some cities receive large amounts of relatively unrestricted funds from other governments to finance activities that other cities are required to fund with local tax revenue. For example, Census Bureau figures show that Rochester received $110 million in 1980 from the state of New York and other local governments (largely from Monroe County), more than twice the amount it received from the federal government and only $15 million less than it raised on its own. By contrast, Tulsa received only $4.3 million from Oklahoma or from other local governments—about 3 percent of its own-source revenue and less than 15 percent of what it received from the federal government. Federal aid is a much larger percentage of local revenue in Rochester than in Tulsa, but this difference may be partly due to the fact that Tulsa finances almost all its budget from its own resources, while Rochester receives substantial funds from other outside sources.

4. For pessimistic assessments drawing on these results, see Roy Bahl, Bernard Jump, Jr., and Larry Schroeder, "The Outlook for City Fiscal Performance in Declining Regions," in Bahl, *Fiscal Outlook;* and John Petersen, "Big City Borrowing Costs and Credit Quality," in Robert Burchell and David Listokin, eds., *Cities Under Stress* (Rutgers University Press, 1981), among others.

2. Functions for which a city is responsible. Metropolitan areas vary widely in the way various functions are divided among different local governments. New York City, for example, is responsible for partial financing of both the aid to families with dependent children (AFDC) and medicaid programs; operates a school system, a city university system, a public housing system, a sewer system, and a park system; and subsidizes both the city transit and hospital systems. In Chicago, by contrast, all of these functions are performed by special districts or by other levels of government for which the city has no direct financial responsibility.[5] These differences affect both the range of activities that cities support with tax revenue and the amount of federal support they receive, since public housing, education, transit, and sewer systems all receive substantial federal support, but are not connected in any simple way to the importance of federal money in city budgets.

3. The level of service the city provides. A city whose citizens want a relatively limited level of services will tax less, and hence appear to be more dependent, than a city receiving the same amount of federal money whose citizens prefer a higher level of city services and are willing to pay for it through higher taxes. As a crude example, New York City supported approximately 150 workers per 10,000 residents in 1978 to provide such basic services as police, fire, and sanitation, while Houston employed only 63 workers for every 10,000 residents to provide the same services. Other things being equal, New York might be expected to have a higher tax level than Houston in order to support this higher level of service. This difference in service levels, however, is not affected in any simple way by the amount of federal money either city receives.

4. The price of providing a given level of service. Differences among cities in prevailing local wages and the costs of equipment, materials, and transportation require some cities to pay more tax money than others to support the same level of service. Environmental Protection Agency figures indicate, for example, that the same sewer would cost 50 percent more to construct in New York than in Houston. Such differences in price levels, like differences in services, affect local taxes, but have no necessary relationship to how important federal money is to the city's budget.

5. The proportion of federal funds a city uses to support its own agencies.

5. For a detailed description of the way these differences in responsibility affect local spending patterns, see Richard P. Nathan and Paul R. Dommel, "The Cities," in Joseph Pechman, ed., *Setting National Priorities: The 1978 Budget* (Brookings Institution, 1977).

Many cities allocated part of their Comprehensive Employment and Training Act (CETA) grants to other local governments or to community-based organizations, and some cities delegated significant portions of community development block grant (CDBG) funds to community groups. Funds treated in this way show up in a city's budget as revenue from the federal government, but because they support no direct city activities it is difficult to argue that their presence constitutes city dependence on federal money.

These differences among cities in the organization and financing of local government indicate that differences in dependence, as currently defined and calculated, may reflect differences in the functions for which cities are responsible or the level of assistance they receive from state governments rather than differences in the importance of grant dollars in local budgets. Current measures of dependence, in short, may produce misleading results about the relative importance of grant dollars in the budgets of different American cities.

Perhaps more important, calculations of this sort do little to reveal the importance of federal funds to city finances because they do not indicate the types of services that cities use federal dollars to support. It is impossible to tell what a city uses federal money for from the overall amount of money it receives, yet knowing how aid is spent is crucial to judging the degree of a city's dependence.

More precisely, cities that rely heavily on federal funds to supply basic or core services can be judged to be more dependent on those funds than those that use the funds for other purposes. Regardless of what else they do, almost all cities provide police and fire protection, pick up garbage, build and maintain city streets and other public infrastructure, and maintain an administrative structure. Even in the most conservative cities, these activities are seen as legitimate functions of city government, enjoy a relatively broad base of support, and are considered to be legitimate claimants on the city budget that should be supported at adequate levels before other services are provided.

By contrast, cities vary widely in the extent to which they provide such services as manpower training or other social services, health services, housing assistance, and cultural activities. These activities are less universally accepted as legitimate city functions, and their base of political support and claim on city resources are less well established than those of the basic services. Hence they are more likely to be dependent on outside resources and more likely to be cut in the event of budget difficulties.

The basic services historically have been financed with locally raised revenue at levels determined by local officials, and have generally been the last services to be cut in the event of financial problems. Use of federal funds to support these services carries the implication that local revenues are not sufficient to maintain these services at minimal levels and that no alternative sources of support exist, since other services have already been reduced.

This formulation suggests that such factors as the condition of the city budget, the attitudes of local decisionmakers and interest groups, and the amount of discretion provided in the use of grants are likely to be the most important determinants of what cities do with federal funds and how dependent they are on these dollars.

Budgetary and Political Context

Most existing models of the allocation of federal grants by state and local governments assume that the use of federal funds is driven by the same forces that influence the allocation of other local revenue. More precisely, most models make two general assumptions about the character of federal money and the political forces that affect its allocation:

1. Local officials view federal dollars in much the same way as local funds, in that there is no risk or uncertainty, either actual or perceived, associated with their continuation;

2. Federal funds are allocated through the same political channels, by the same actors, and in response to the same set of political constraints as other sources of revenue.[6]

6. Most such models rely either on extensions of consumer choice theory in which the median local voter is the effective decisionmaker or on simulations of the allocation of resources among various functions that local governments perform. While clear statements of these assumptions are rare, neither set of models explicitly incorporates the possibility of either actual or perceived uncertainty associated with federal funds, and both explain the allocation of federal funds in terms of the same factors that influence the use of local funds—the preferences of the median voter in one case and standing decision rules about the division of additional funds between local functions in the other. See, for example, Paul Courant, Edward Gramlich and Daniel Rubinfeld, "The Stimulative Effects of Intergovernmental Grants: Or Why Money Sticks Where It Hits," in Peter Mieszkowski and William Oakland, eds., *Fiscal Federalism and Grants-in-Aid* (Urban Institute, 1979); and Patrick D. Larkey, *Evaluating Public Programs: The Impact of General Revenue Sharing on Municipal Government* (Princeton University Press, 1979). Larkey recognizes the possibility of risk-averse behavior and allocation of federal funds outside the normal budget process, but gives no indication of how his results would be modified in either of these cases.

This essay assumes, to the contrary, that unless they have pressing reasons to do so, elected officials (1) will not pump large amounts of federal money into local operating budgets, because of uncertainty related to federal aid, and (2) will not become closely involved in allocating federal funds among competing uses and beneficiaries, because of the political risks involved in doing so.

Uncertain Funding Levels

The most important reason for uncertainty is the possibility of cuts in funding levels. With the exception of general revenue sharing, all major federal urban aid programs are subject to the annual appropriations process and all have relatively short authorization periods (in most cases three years or less). Some education programs are "forward funded"—that is, funds are appropriated a year before they are spent—but for most federal programs both the amount of money available and the terms under which these funds are available are subject to frequent unpredictable changes.

These changes can have a substantial impact on city budgets. When Congress let the economic stimulus package expire in 1978, for example, some cities lost aid amounting to more than 10 percent of local tax revenues. At the same time, Congress imposed new restrictions on the eligibility, wages, and tenure of participants in the public service employment (PSE) program that made it much harder to use these funds to support regular city services. Local governments that had used these funds to support normal city activities were required to reduce services to match cuts, increase local taxes to continue services, or invest time and effort lobbying the Department of Labor for waivers of the new PSE requirements.[7]

Regulatory Requirements

A second source of uncertainty for local officials is enforcement of rules governing uses and beneficiaries of federal funds. Grant programs adopted during the seventies reduced federal influence over local decisions, but

7. For a description of these changes, see Richard P. Nathan and James W. Fossett, "Targeted Fiscal Assistance," in *Targeted Fiscal Assistance to State and Local Governments*, Hearings before the Subcommittee on Revenue Sharing, Intergovernmental Revenue Impact, and Economic Problems of the Senate Committee on Finance, 96 Cong. 1. sess. (GPO, 1979), pp. 58–72; and William Mirengoff and others, *The New CETA: Effects on Public Service Employment Problems* (U.S. Department of Labor, 1980).

federal agencies still interpret and enforce regulations on such matters as participant and project eligibility, as well as affirmative action and environmental impact requirements. Federal agency "signals" to local governments about what is and is not permissible under particular programs and the strength with which these signals are enforced are important variables in determining local use of funds.

These "signals" are, however, also subject to change. Congressional complaints, adverse media coverage, and changes in federal agency personnel can cause sudden shifts. The community development block grant program is a case in point. Under the Ford administration, the Department of Housing and Urban Development (HUD) allowed local governments considerable freedom to decide what types of programs would be funded and which areas of cities would be eligible to benefit. When the Carter administration began, new officials at HUD adopted regulations requiring local governments to spend the bulk of CDBG funds on activities that would primarily benefit low- and moderate-income groups. This change in agency signals forced some local governments to alter geographic spending patterns substantially and to change the types of activities they supported with CDBG funds.[8] More recently, the Reagan administration has abolished most of the Carter regulations, once again allowing local governments to spend CDBG money as they please.

Uncertainty about the level and form of federal aid makes local officials hesitant to use substantial amounts of federal money in the city's operating budget. In the event of funding cutbacks or significant rule changes, officials would be forced to choose between raising local taxes or reducing services, thus alienating either local taxpayers or recipients of federally funded services. Officials naturally want to avoid such a situation.

Political Control and Utilization

Gaining political control over federally funded programs is also potentially risky for local elected officials. Federal funds do provide jobs and contracts that can be used as a political resource to reward supporters as well as to provide services at no cost to local taxpayers. Nevertheless, mayors and council members have reason to avoid taking an active role in the management of federally supported programs.

8. See Paul R. Dommel and others, *Targeting Community Development* (U.S. Department of Housing and Urban Development, 1980), chaps. 1, 6.

Three considerations help account for this reluctance. First, the uncertainty of federal funding may make it unwise to use federal funds as a means of generating or maintaining political support through patronage or award of contracts. Funding cutbacks or changes in regulations may leave officials with more claimants than they can satisfy with local funds. As a result, local officials may wish to avoid creating expectations that they may not be able to fulfill in the future.

Second, involvement with some federally funded programs may attract opposition from politically important groups. Some groups view public service employment as "make-work" or "leaf raking" or object to the subsidized housing requirements attached to the CDBG program. In many cities, the risk of generating such opposition may be greater than the potential benefits that a local official would gain by becoming involved in these programs. While the community development and CETA programs have increased the incentive for representatives of minorities and disadvantaged groups to participate in electoral politics by channeling grants to city hall rather than to community groups, many such groups may still lack the ability to deliver votes or other support to elected officials in exchange for program funding. In cities where party systems are relatively weak, political participation has been historically low, or most officials are elected at large, representatives of minority groups may have found it inordinately difficult to develop a base of support that would enable them to bargain effectively with local elected officials. In such cases, local officials have little incentive to devote much attention to the operation of federally funded programs, since the return in electoral or other support is likely to be small.

Finally, regulations governing the use of federal funds may not provide enough discretion to provide political benefits for local officials in allocation decisions. All cities are subject to the same regulations, but those regulations have different effects in different cities. For example, the Carter administration's regulations requiring cities to concentrate CDBG spending in low- and moderate-income areas defined "low and moderate income" by reference to the median income of the entire metropolitan area. As a result, cities with high median incomes relative to their suburbs were more restricted in where they could spend CDBG funds than were the poor cities. In the cities with high median incomes, relatively few officials had an opportunity to benefit politically from the allocation of federal funds, and few neighborhood groups were interested in how and where these funds were spent. As a result, there was little incentive for local officials to become actively involved in the allocation of these dollars.

Minimizing Political Risks

In short, the level and form of federal funds cannot be accurately forecast from one year to the next, and the political costs associated with public involvement with federal funds may be substantial and the benefits minimal. It is reasonable, therefore, to expect local officials to be extremely cautious about relying on these dollars either as support for ongoing city activities or as a source of political capital.

Local officials are likely to use any or all of several approaches that minimize political risks involved in use of federal funds. They may allocate those funds outside the normal budget process or spend them primarily for capital projects or nonrecurring operating expenses that could be discontinued with little trouble. Elected officials may also put some political distance between themselves and federal programs by allowing program staffs to make most major decisions about where to spend federal aid. Delegating these decisions allows elected officials to avoid being identified with federally funded activities by groups opposed to them and makes them less vulnerable to demands to continue federally supported programs if these funds were to be terminated.

Description of Case Studies

In order to investigate the impact of federal funds on local finances and politics in a fashion that provides evidence on what cities have used federal dollars to support and the ways in which these dollars have affected local politics, field associates of the Brookings Institution conducted a series of case studies on the impact of federal grants in eleven large cities as of 1978. The studies were made under contract between Brookings and the U.S. Departments of Labor and Commerce. The cities selected for examination, described in table 1, vary widely in rates of population and economic growth, financial condition, political structure and culture, experience with earlier federal programs, and most other characteristics that might be expected to affect their use of federal funds. The authors of the studies are locally based economists and political scientists selected by a central staff at Brookings for their knowledge of city finances and politics. All had participated in earlier field network evaluation studies of the general

Table 1. *Population, Urban Conditions, and Economic Growth in Case Study Cities*

City	1977 population	Urban conditions index, 1975[a]	Percentage change in			
			Value added, manufacturing, 1972–76	Retail sales, 1972–77	Wholesale sales, 1972–77	Selected service receipts, 1972–77
New York	7,257,787	222	3.9	14.7	64.1	8.2
Chicago	3,062,881	255	22.8	19.5	33.2	18.7
Los Angeles	2,761,222	89	49.3	49.3	76.3	59.2
Houston	1,554,960	40	85.5	85.5	n.a.	158.1
Detroit	1,289,910	266	24.8	9.0	12.5	−17.3
Phoenix	864,516	21	50.5	56.9	69.8	58.2
Boston	618,493	303	15.8	12.5	19.3	37.5
Cleveland	609,187	400	28.8	17.4	16.8	14.6
St. Louis	517,671	487	37.8	17.5	73.0	12.8
Tulsa	334,365	57	62.4	62.4	n.a.	62.6
Rochester	256,285	266	32.5	5.7	−7.7	34.6

Sources: Population: U.S. Bureau of the Census, *City Government Finances in 1977–78* (Government Printing Office, 1980); urban conditions index: Paul R. Dommel, *Decentralizing Community Development* (GPO, 1979), appendix II; 1972–1976/77 figures: James W. Fossett and Richard P. Nathan, "The Prospects for Urban Revival," in Roy Bahl, ed., *Urban Government Finances: Emerging Trends* (Sage Publications, 1981).
    n.a. Not available.
    a. The urban conditions index is a three-factor index that combines population and concentration of older housing and poverty. The mean of this index is standardized at 100. Cities with index scores above 100 are more distressed than the average; those with scores below 100 are less distressed.

revenue-sharing, public service employment, and community development block grant programs.[9] The case studies were prepared according to a common analytical framework developed jointly by the central staff and the field associates, which consists of four basic sets of questions:

1. To what extent have cities become dependent on federal funds to pay for basic services? As argued earlier, the total amount of federal aid a city receives provides little indication of the services it uses federal dollars to support or of the city's ability to continue financing these services if funds were discontinued. Use of federal funds to support basic city services is a better indicator of city dependence on federal money than the total amount of such funds the city receives.

These case studies use a variety of approaches to determine the extent

9. For a description of these studies, see Richard P. Nathan, "The Methodology for Field Network Evaluation Studies," in Walter Williams, ed., *Studying Implementation* (Chatham, N.J.: Chatham House, 1981).

to which a city is dependent on federal funds. Each case study reports not only on the share of the city budget supported by federal dollars, but also on the services supported by those dollars and local ability and willingness to continue the activities supported by federal money if these funds were discontinued. Because it deals not only with how much money a city gets but also with what the city would do if aid were curtailed, this approach provides a broader view than other studies of the political and financial importance of federal grants to cities.

2. What was the impact of the Carter administration's economic stimulus package on local finances and unemployment levels? All three programs in the package were designed to increase employment and enhance local recovery from the recession of 1973–75, but through very different approaches. The antirecession fiscal assistance program provided funds to local governments in areas of high unemployment to pay employee salaries, with the intent of preventing governments from responding to revenue losses by laying off personnel. The local public works program attempted to stimulate employment in the construction industry by providing grants for construction and rehabilitation of public facilities. The public service employment (PSE) program provided public jobs to long-term unemployed persons through grants to state and local governments, which could hire individuals on their own payrolls or subcontract hiring to community organizations or other governments.

All three of these programs had been enacted under the Ford administration, but were roughly doubled in size when reenacted or extended in 1977. The Carter administration's attempts to convert the programs into permanent, structurally oriented programs when the stimulus package expired in 1978 were unsuccessful. These case studies assess the effectiveness of the programs in promoting local economic and budgetary recovery, describe the advantages and disadvantages of each program as it was operated locally, and indicate some of the results of the programs' termination or reduction.

3. Who benefits from federally supported programs? Federal programs vary widely in the extent to which they regulate the types of services local governments can provide with federal funds and the income groups or areas which can receive these services. Some federal programs, such as the school lunch program operated by the Department of Agriculture, require local governments to spend federal money on specified services for particular income groups or areas; others specify who must be served, but allow local governments to decide how to serve them; still other

programs define the service to be provided, but impose no restrictions on beneficiaries. These case studies report on which income groups in each city are the major direct beneficiaries of the programs supported by federal funds, using a common method for classifying benefits to different groups in the population. The studies identify the major political and programmatic factors that influence the distribution of benefits.

4. Who decides how federal money will be spent? As noted earlier, grant programs adopted in the seventies were designed to take decision-making power about the use of federal funds away from appointed officials and give it to elected officials such as mayors and legislators. This redistribution of power was to be achieved by making grants to city governments rather than to special authorities or nongovernmental organizations and by requiring both the mayor and the city council to approve proposed uses of funds.

While these procedural changes provide elected officials with considerable potential influence over how federal funds are allocated, they do not ensure that mayors and councils will, in fact, exercise that potential. Officials in some cities may choose, for reasons suggested earlier, not to involve themselves actively in these decisions, allowing professional staffs and concerned interest groups to determine how federal funds are to be allocated. These case studies describe the political process by which federal money is allocated in each city, identify the actors and groups that have played major roles in this process, and assess how federal grants have affected local decisionmaking and politics.

Remeasuring Dependence

Table 2 shows the total amount of funds that the eleven cities received and spent in 1978, divided between operating and capital purposes. Table 3 displays different measures of dependence on federal funds spent for operating purposes. Column 1 of table 3 displays the size of federal operating funds as a percentage of local tax revenue, which has been frequently reported as a measure of dependence. These figures suggest conditions not dissimilar from those reported by other observers—extensive reliance on federal funds as a source of operating support. On average, the amount of federal aid these cities used for operating purposes in 1978 was equal to 43.3 percent of city tax revenues. In seven cities federal funds were equivalent to over 40 percent of local tax revenues, and in three—Phoenix, Cleveland, and Detroit—this figure was more than 50 percent. Based on

Table 2. *Federal Aid by Type, Fiscal Year 1978*
Thousands of dollars

City	Carryover obligations and allocations from FY 1977	Federal obligations and allocations, FY 1978	Total federal aid available, FY 1978	Federal aid funds expenditures, FY 1978	Carryover obligations and allocations to FY 1979
Detroit					
Operating	68,948	122,504	191,252	176,225	14,911
Capital	114,893	72,146	187,039	75,817	110,166
Total	183,841	194,650	382,291	252,042	125,077
Phoenix					
Operating	3,934	61,960	65,894	66,200	(306)
Capital	n.a.	27,230	27,230	23,978	3,252
Total	3,934	89,190	93,124	90,178	2,946
Los Angeles					
Operating	n.a.	n.a.	347,589	274,898	72,691
Capital	n.a.	n.a.	198,045	38,036	160,009
Total	n.a.	n.a.	545,634	312,934	232,700
Tulsa					
Operating	3,408	18,862	22,310	20,682	1,588
Capital	4,877	6,965	11,843	4,560	7,283
Total	8,285	25,826	34,153	25,242	8,970
Rochester					
Operating	422	26,293	26,716	23,529	n.a.
Capital	15,952	19,923	35,875	17,297	n.a.
Total	16,375	46,216	62,590	40,826	n.a.
Chicago					
Operating	86,674	522,766	609,440	332,238	277,202
Capital	136,399	155,782	292,181	91,762	200,419
Total	223,073	678,548	901,621	424,000	477,621
Boston					
Operating	n.a.	n.a.	n.a.	156,778	n.a.
Capital	n.a.	n.a.	n.a.	38,497	n.a.
Total	n.a.	n.a.	n.a.	195,275	n.a.

these figures, most, if not all, of these cities would have to be judged as dependent on federal funds.

The next two columns of table 3 show the fraction of federal operating funds spent on basic services and the amount of local expenditures on basic services accounted for by federal dollars.[10] These figures suggest both a

10. As used here, "basic services" includes those activities corresponding to the Census Bureau's expenditure categories of public safety, public works, sanitation, and general administration. Education has also been included as a basic service for New York and Boston, since both cities operate the local school system as a city department, and its political claim on the city budget in these cities is as strong as that of other departments that provide services more commonly labeled as basic.

Table 2 *(continued)*

Thousands of dollars

City	Carryover obligations and allocations from FY 1977	Federal obligations and allocations, FY 1978	Total federal aid available, FY 1978	Federal aid funds expenditures, FY 1978	Carryover obligations and allocations to FY 1979
St. Louis					
Operating	24,440	74,646	99,086	67,754	31,332
Capital	18,235	43,373	61,608	15,452	46,156
Total	42,675	118,019	160,694	83,206	77,488
Cleveland					
Operating	n.a.	n.a.	n.a.	67,541	n.a.
Capital	n.a.	n.a.	n.a.	14,028	n.a.
Total	n.a.	n.a.	n.a.	81,569	n.a.
Houston					
Operating	49,437	70,262	119,699	84,681	35,018
Capital	119,939	140,356	332,296	126,101	206,194
Total	241,377	210,618	451,995	210,782	241,213
New York[a]					
Operating	n.a.	n.a.	1,219,700	1,199,700	20,000
Capital	n.a.	n.a.	2,079,400	423,900	1,655,500
Total	n.a.	n.a.	3,299,100	1,623,600	1,675,500

Sources: Thomas J. Anton, *Federal Aid to Detroit* (Brookings Institution, 1983); Sarah F. Liebschutz, *Federal Aid to Rochester* (Brookings Institution, 1984); Charles J. Orlebeke, *Federal Aid to Chicago* (Brookings Institution, 1983); Henry J. Schmandt, George D. Wendel, and E. Allan Tomey, *Federal Aid to St. Louis* (Brookings Institution, 1983); Susan A. MacManus, *Federal Aid to Houston* (Brookings Institution, 1983); John S. Hall, *The Impact of Federal Grants on the City of Phoenix* (U.S. Departments of Labor and Commerce, Report MEL 79-25[3], October 1979); Ruth Ross, *The Impact of Federal Grants on the City of Los Angeles* (U.S. Departments of Labor and Commerce, Report MEL 80-21, November 1980); Steve B. Steib and R. Lynn Rittenoure, *The Impact of Federal Grants on the City of Tulsa* (U.S. Departments of Labor and Commerce, Report MEL 80-05, March 1980); Jonathan Katz, *The Impact of Federal Grants on the City of Boston* (U.S. Departments of Labor and Commerce, Report MEL 80-15, October 1980); Richard F. Tompkins and others, *The Impact of Federal Grants on the City of Cleveland* (U.S. Departments of Labor and Commerce, Report MEL 81-19, February 1981); and Julia Vitullo-Martin, "The Impact of Federal Grants on New York City, FY 1972–FY 1978" (n.p., May 1981).

n.a. Not available.

a. Excludes AFDC, medicaid, and title XX of the Social Security Act, which finances the provision of social services to AFDC recipients and is operated by county governments in other jurisdictions.

lower level of dependence on federal funds overall and a very different distribution of reliance on federal funds than suggested by the figures in the first column. Although total federal aid for operating purposes amounts to a large share of city finances if measured against local taxes, less than 40 percent of the money was used to fund departments that provide basic services. This portion of the aid amounted to, on average, less than 20 percent of city expenditures for these services. Neither of these fractions is negligible, but they do suggest that city dependence on federal money, at least over this period, was considerably lower than prevailing wisdom might suggest.

Perhaps more important, these figures suggest that the amount of federal

Table 3. *Three Measures of Dependence on Federal Funds, 1978*

City	Federal operating grants as percentage of local taxes	Percentage of federal operating grants spent on basic services[a]	Federal operating grants for basic services as percentage of total spending on basic services
Phoenix	66.0	30.2	14.7
Cleveland	58.4	46.0	24.0
Detroit	52.4	49.0[b]	25.5[b]
Chicago	49.6	28.7	10.9
St. Louis	44.0	49.9[b]	27.0[b]
Los Angeles	41.6	10.3	4.5
Tulsa	40.1	18.3	11.3
Rochester	36.8	92.4	22.3
Boston	36.4	39.3	13.0
Houston	31.0	16.5	4.4
New York[c]	19.5	55.3	22.7
Average	43.3	39.6	16.4

Sources: Same as table 2.
a. Basic services include public safety, public works, sanitation, and general administration. For New York and Boston, schools have also been added.
b. Estimated on the basis of employment.
c. Excludes AFDC and medicaid from federal funds received.

money a city receives relative to its own taxes has little relationship to the city's propensity to spend those funds on basic services. Of the five cities with above-average ratios of aid to tax revenues, only three—Cleveland, Detroit, and St. Louis—spent greater than average shares of these funds on basic services. Three other cities—Rochester, Boston, and New York—spent substantial amounts of federal money to support basic services but received smaller than average amounts of aid relative to local taxes. By contrast, several cities, such as Phoenix and Chicago, received large amounts of federal funds relative to their own taxes but spent smaller than average fractions of these funds for basic services. Put simply, the amount of federal money a city receives tells next to nothing about what the city does with the money.

Explaining Grant Politics

Local officials' inability to predict how much federal revenue will be available from year to year and the restrictions on its use create strong incentives for them to spend federal money for activities that could be discontinued without establishing a permanent claim on the city budget or to allocate it outside the normal budget process altogether by leaving decisions about its use to program staff.

In some cities, however, these incentives may have been ineffective. In these cities, mayors and councils have been actively involved in allocating federal funds, and substantial amounts have been used to support basic city services. Three factors appear to distinguish those cities where federal dollars have become politically and financially important from those where these funds have been allocated largely by staff outside the normal budget process. These factors are (1) the city's financial condition, (2) the degree of discretion the city has in deciding how to allocate federal money, and (3) the level of political organization in the city, combined with attitudes of city officials toward federal money.

Financial Condition

The most important of these factors has been the city's financial condition. Cities with relatively few financial problems are likely to use federal aid cautiously. These cities can adequately support normal city services from their own resources, so they can afford to insulate themselves from the uncertainty surrounding federal funds by using them for activities that create no permanent claim on the city budget. One might expect that such cities would use large amounts of federal dollars to support such activities as social services or expansion of maintenance and cleanup activities of various sorts. Some such cities may delegate federally funded activities to other governments or community groups as much as possible. Because officials in these cities wish to avoid any political claim on city funds if federal programs are discontinued, they are likely to allocate little city money to the activities supported by federal dollars.

In cities with more severe financial problems, officials might be expected to adopt a different attitude toward the appropriate uses of federal money. If local revenues are not sufficient to cover desired levels of expenditures on such services as police, fire, and streets, then local officials are unlikely to be able to afford caution. Using federal funds to expand social services or other secondary activities while laying off police officers or fire fighters would make local officials vulnerable to attack both from organized municipal employees and from voters who support the continuation of basic services but are less enthusiastic about expanding social services. Because the beneficiaries of social services may be less well organized and thus less able to obtain separate treatment for the funds that provide these services, local officials in hard-pressed cities may find it expedient to use federal funds as a source of support for ongoing basic city activities.

The uncertainty of federal aid is less likely to concern officials in cities with a high degree of fiscal pressure, because they already are likely to be living from budget to budget. For these officials, the immediate problem of balancing the current year's accounts is likely to take precedence over the future problem of possible cuts in federal funds. Moreover, if federal funds are withdrawn, these officials can convincingly plead poverty and eliminate federally supported programs with less political risk than officials in more prosperous cities. Because federal dollars are probably the most significant source of uncommitted revenue available in hard-pressed cities, officials in these cities have reason to use these dollars to maintain ongoing city services and even to lobby federal officials to relax regulations against using grant money for these purposes.

Persistent shortages of city revenue also affect the politics surrounding the budget process. As students of organization theory have frequently argued, decisions on how to allocate resources are made at a higher level in the organizational hierarchy when resources are scarce than when there is plenty of slack. Because there are fewer resources to satisfy competing demands, higher levels of authority must be invoked to decide how resources will be divided.[11] This argument suggests that mayors and city budget officials in hard-pressed cities will spend more time trying to control expenditures and to locate additional sources of revenue than their counterparts in more prosperous places. For example, decisions on whether or not to fill vacant positions would be made by department heads in more prosperous places, but in hard-pressed cities these decisions are more likely to be made by central budget staff or through mayorally imposed guidelines.

Fiscal pressure also creates a strong incentive for mayors and budget officials to create slack by centralizing control over the allocation of discretionary revenue, including federal funds. Over the period under consideration here, for example, the law imposed virtually no limits on the number of laid-off city employees that a city could hire with public service employment funds, the length of time a PSE worker could stay in the

---

11. See, for example, Michael Cohen, James March, and Johan P. Olson, "A Garbage Can Model of Organizational Choice," *Administrative Science Quarterly*, vol. 17 (March 1972), pp. 1–25.

program, or the salary that could be paid participants. In this situation, cities could relatively easily convert PSE funds into a source of support for ongoing city activities. Therefore, one might expect that mayors and budget officials of hard-pressed cities would be more involved in the allocation of these funds than their counterparts in more prosperous places, and that hard-pressed cities would be more likely to use PSE funds to support normal city services.[12]

Although classifying a city's financial condition is difficult to do precisely, the cities under consideration here can be divided with some confidence into two groups of roughly equal size. Over the mid-1970s, New York, Cleveland, Detroit, St. Louis, Rochester, and Boston operated under relatively stringent financial conditions, while Chicago, Los Angeles, Houston, Tulsa, and Phoenix were under relatively less pressure. This division is based on the relative rates of growth in revenues and expenditures and on the relative conditions of general funds.

As the figures in table 1 suggest, economic growth in the cities classified as hard-pressed was substantially slower than in the more prosperous places. Value added by manufacturing grew by an average of 24 percent in the hard-pressed cities, compared with 54 percent in the cities classified as more prosperous. Differences in growth rates in retail sales and service receipts were equally substantial. As a result of these disparities, the more prosperous cities realized substantial growth in local revenues and city employment, while the budgets of harder-pressed cities grew at a slower rate in spite of increases, some major, in local tax rates. On average, general fund revenues grew at an annual average rate of almost 14 percent between 1973 and 1978 in the more prosperous cities, while revenues in the hard-pressed cities grew less than half as fast. Noneducational employment by city governments, including jobs supported by federal funds, grew by an average of 25 percent over this period in the cities classified as prosperous, while city employment declined by an average of 8 percent in the hard-pressed places.

Not surprisingly, these two groups of cities also showed substantial differences in the condition of their general funds. The condition of this fund can be measured in two ways. The first, shown in table 4, measures over the city fiscal year income to and expenditures from the general fund relative to total general fund expenditures. These figures indicate that the

12. See Janet Galchick, "Local Variations in Implementing Public Service Employment: An Analysis of Process and Outcomes" (Princeton Urban and Regional Research Center, 1981), for a more detailed statement of this argument.

Table 4. *General Fund Revenue Excess or Deficiency as Percentage of General Fund Expenditures, 1973–78*

City	1973	1974	1975	1976	1977	1978
Hard-pressed cities						
New York	−7.2	−15.6	n.a.	−28.2	−26.8	−8.0
Detroit	11.2	1.4	−4.5	−3.1	9.3	−3.6
Cleveland[a]	n.a.	−0.1	0.2	0.1	−0.2	n.a.
Boston	n.a.	n.a.	−0.6	−9.0	3.9	−2.3
St. Louis	−4.0	−6.3	8.5	1.4	1.1	2.7
More prosperous cities						
Chicago	7.4	7.4	−0.1	0.5	2.7	−2.0
Los Angeles	−2.3	10.1	2.2	2.1	0.3	5.2
Houston	−3.9	6.0	3.2	1.4	1.7	−3.0
Phoenix	−0.8	−3.1	−0.7	2.3	3.7	−0.5

Sources: Philip M. Dearborn, *Elements of Municipal Financial Analysis: Parts I–V* (Boston: First Boston Corporation, 1975); Dearborn, "The Financial Health of Major U.S. Cities in 1978 (Washington, D.C.: Urban Institute, 1979); and unpublished data. Comparable information was not available for Tulsa or Rochester.

n.a. Not available.

a. As reported. Subsequent audits have indicated larger deficits.

cities classified as hard-pressed ran larger and more frequent revenue deficiencies over this period than more prosperous places. All of the hard-pressed cities had a deficiency at least twice over this period, and three of them raised less than they spent in three or more years. The average deficiency was almost 8 percent of general fund expenditures. Even excluding New York, which experienced a major financial crisis over this period, the hard-pressed cities had more frequent and larger deficits than the more prosperous cities. While all but one of the cities classified as more prosperous showed revenue deficiencies in at least two years, only Phoenix showed a deficiency in three or more years, and the average size of these deficiencies was less than one-fourth that of the hard-pressed cities.

The second way to judge the condition of city general funds is to measure the fund's surplus or deficit at the end of each fiscal year. A current-year deficiency may be the result of unanticipated revenue shortfalls or increased expenditures and not a symptom of any major problem if the government has an adequate level of current assets available as a budget reserve. Table 5 displays the difference between general fund assets (such as cash and investments) and liabilities (such as outstanding debts) for each city, again expressed as a percentage of general fund expenditures. Because these cities vary widely in the types of holdings they can count as assets, balances

Table 5. *General Fund Surplus or Deficit as Percentage of General Fund Expenditures, 1973–78*

Pro forma cash basis

City	1973	1974	1975	1976	1977	1978
Hard-pressed cities						
New York	−7.2	−16.6	n.a.	−28.2	−26.8	−8.1
Detroit	4.4	4.4	0.1	−5.5	4.0	−4.2
Cleveland	0.1	n.a.	0.1	0.3	0.1	n.a.
Boston	n.a.	n.a.	−0.4	−4.7	−4.5	−9.5
St. Louis	−2.8	−8.6	−0.2	1.2	0.1	2.9
More prosperous cities						
Chicago[a]	−36.0	−29.0	−25.0	−24.9	−21.2	−22.6
Los Angeles	23.5	39.6	27.0	21.5	17.7	22.4
Houston	3.3	6.3	7.6	7.5	8.4	3.8
Phoenix	4.7	0.5	1.5	3.0	8.3	9.5

Sources: Same as table 4.
n.a. Not available.
a. See text for explanation of Chicago's deficits.

and deficits have been recalculated on a pro forma cash basis, which adjusts for the way these cities handle assets.

The cities classified here as hard-pressed showed larger and more frequent deficits on this measure than the cities rated as more prosperous. The only city in the latter group that showed *any* general deficit—Chicago—did so because of state accounting requirements for handling property taxes, rather than because of any severe financial problems.[13] Not only do the cities classified as hard-pressed run more frequent deficits on a current-year basis, but also they are less well protected from potential adverse developments such as economic downturns or unanticipated expenditures.

If the argument here is correct, these two groups of cities should have used federal money for different purposes. Cities classified as prosperous might be expected to use limited amounts of federal dollars to support ongoing city activities, preferring instead to concentrate these funds in activities that could be easily terminated if federal funds were discontinued. In cities classified as hard-pressed, federal funds should support a larger share of the city budget in general and of basic city services in particular. In brief, the hard-pressed cities should be more politically and financially dependent on federal funds.

13. For a more detailed discussion of this problem, see Philip Dearborn, "The Financial Health of Major U.S. Cities in 1978" (Washington, D.C.: Urban Institute, 1979).

Discretion

The second factor that appears to affect how cities allocate federal money and how they spend it is the amount of discretion they have in using it. While all cities are subject to the same set of regulations governing the expenditure of federal money, these regulations confer different degrees of discretion on different cities. The most striking example of this difference in discretion occurs in the CDBG program. Regulations promulgated during the Carter administration required cities to spend the bulk of these funds in areas of low or moderate income, but defined "low and moderate income" by reference to the median family income of the entire metropolitan area rather than to that of the city. As a result, cities with high median incomes relative to their suburbs were more restricted in where they could spend CDBG funds than were cities whose median income is low relative to their surrounding areas. The former cities could spend CDBG money in relatively few "pockets of poverty"; the latter cities could spend it in any or all of a large number of neighborhoods.

Variations in discretion might be expected to affect both the level of political interest in the allocation of federal money and the income groups that benefit from these dollars. If cities have little discretion in where they can spend federal funds, then relatively few elected officials have a potential stake in the allocation of these dollars and relatively few interest groups are likely to be concerned about where funds are spent. As a result, decisions about what to do with federal dollars are likely to be made by program staff, who may be more likely to focus these funds on the lower-income areas of the city, either because they agree with the federal policy of targeting funds or because they lack the political resources to resist these directives. If, on the other hand, large areas of the city are eligible to receive federal dollars, then there will be more elected officials and interest groups with a potential interest in how funds are spent. Decisions about what to do with federal funds are more likely to be made by elected officials and benefits are likely to be more dispersed geographically than in cities where discretion is more limited.

Among the cities under consideration, geographic discretion was most limited in the three cities in the Southwest—Phoenix, Houston, and Tulsa—all of which have high incomes relative to their suburbs. In Phoenix, for example, fewer than 25 percent of the census tracts had median family incomes in 1970 that qualified as "low and moderate income." John Hall argues:

A substantial portion of the total CDBG expenditure since the start of the grant has been concentrated in the South Phoenix and inner city areas. Because so many of the city's low-income citizens reside in this area, it is difficult to avoid choosing it as a target for income-tested funds. Unlike harder pressed cities, Phoenix cannot meet income qualifications and still spread funds. Many neighborhoods would not be eligible.[14]

Similar situations were reported by case study authors in both Houston and Tulsa. Since both cities have high median incomes, most federal program funds with income-targeting criteria attached have to be spent in relatively small poor areas of these cities—North Tulsa and the "Fifth Ward" in Houston. In 1970 fewer than one-third of the census tracts in these cities had median family incomes that would qualify as low or moderate. This presumably produced a relatively low level of participation in allocation decisions by elected officials, and a relatively high concentration of the benefits from federal funding in the poorer areas of the city.

The other cities under consideration had greater discretion in the spending of federal funds. Most of these cities have low median incomes relative to their suburbs, so larger shares of the city met federally imposed income criteria. On average, almost half of the census tracts in these cities had median family incomes in 1970 that qualified as low or moderate, suggesting that participation by political officials should be greater in these cities and the dispersion of the benefits from federal dollars should be greater than in the three southwestern cities.

Constituent Organization and Official Attitudes

The third factor that might be expected to affect how these cities spent federal grants can be broadly described as the level of organization and activity in the city's political system. Students of urban politics have argued that cities vary widely in their level of political organization and participation and in the extent to which local officials have incentives to provide services for constituents in order to maintain or enhance their political position. In cities where party, neighborhood, or other sorts of political organizations are relatively well established, voter turnout is relatively high, and local politics are relatively visible, elected officials have a much stronger incen-

14. John S. Hall, *The Impact of Federal Grants on the City of Phoenix* (U.S. Departments of Labor and Commerce, Report MEL 79-25 [3], October 1979), p. 61.

tive to worry about retaining their current office or advancing to a higher one than in cities where levels of political organization and participation are lower. Political conflict and competition are more frequent and more intense in cities with higher levels of political organization, creating a relatively strong incentive for elected officials to actively cultivate constituents and do things to keep them happy.

In cities where political organization and participation are lower, officials are under less pressure to develop and maintain constituencies. Because turnout in elections is relatively low and interest groups are relatively inactive between elections, officials can gain and keep elected office relatively easily without being required to do things to maintain their relationships with electoral coalitions.[15]

The consequences of this distinction for the politics surrounding federal funds are straightforward. In some cities, the potential beneficiaries of federal funds are politically organized and in a position to press council members or mayors to overturn unfavorable staff recommendations or to ensure that their interests are protected. Officials in such cities are more likely to involve themselves in decisions about federal money than are their counterparts in cities where beneficiaries are less well organized and have fewer ties to elected officials. In the latter type of city, the influence of client groups is likely to be limited to formal citizen participation mechanisms required by conditions attached to the grants themselves or to informal influence that the groups have developed with program staff. Other things being equal, active involvement by political officials in decisions about federal money is much more likely in more organized cities than in less organized ones, where such decisions are more likely to be left to program staff.

Among the cities under consideration here, the major division along this dimension that can be made with any confidence is again between Phoenix, Houston, and Tulsa and the other eight cities. Political organization and participation are appreciably lower in these three cities than in the eight others, and local politics are much less visible. As a result, elected officials are less publicly active than in the other cities under consideration. As Hall argues in the case of Phoenix:

Bland politics are the norm for Phoenix. Turnout for Phoenix city elections seldom exceeds 30 percent of the eligible voters, and incumbent council members often

15. For statements of this difference, see Jeffrey Pressman, *Federal Programs and City Politics* (University of California Press, 1975); and Kenneth Prewitt, "Political Ambitions, Voluntarism, and Electoral Accountability," *American Political Science Review*, vol. 64 (March 1970), pp. 5–17.

run very low-profile campaigns without serious opposition. Most successful candidates have been Republicans and have supported such positions as a "business approach to government" and a city council composed of amateur politicians who act as a "board of directors" of city government.

Together with other factors, Hall comments, "This situation has led—perhaps inevitably—to a large role for the professional managers and staffs of the city . . . government."[16]

Similar levels of political activity were identified in both Tulsa and Houston. Elected officials in these three cities tend to have little prior experience before their election to office, to be elected in relatively low-profile campaigns, to conduct public business in settings that attract relatively little public attention, and generally to hold beliefs that stress the limited role of government and the avoidance of public conflict.[17] Under these circumstances, elected officials would be less likely to attempt to influence the use of federal money or to view these funds as a potential resource that might be used toward the furtherance of other goals.

In the other eight cities under consideration, levels of political organization and participation are much higher, creating a stronger incentive for elected officials to actively solicit and maintain constituencies to keep them in office. These cities differ widely in the formal and informal distribution of power, the types of interest groups that attend local politics, and practically every other aspect of local political activity. All, however, maintain a sufficient level of participation and competition to induce elected officials to engage in overtly "political" behavior. By contrast with their colleagues in the three southwestern cities, elected officials in these cities are more likely to have political experience before their election to office, to be elected in campaigns that attract at least minimal levels of public attention, and to conduct business in settings that are relatively visible and often involve substantial public conflict. One might expect, therefore, more active involvement in these cities by elected officials in decisions about what to do with federal funds and higher levels of conflict surrounding these decisions.

Three Levels of Dependence

These three factors—financial condition, discretion, and levels of political organization and activity—divide the cities under consideration into

16. Hall, *Phoenix*, pp. 13, 14; and John Hall, "Epilogue" (n.p., 1981).

17. See the essays on all three of these cities in Leonard Goodall, ed., *Urban Politics in the Southwest* (Arizona State University Press, 1967).

three groups reflecting differences in political and financial dependence. The first group of cities is those classified as hard-pressed: New York, Cleveland, Detroit, St. Louis, Rochester, and Boston. In these cities, all three factors create strong incentives for federal funds to be allocated through normal budgetary channels and for substantial amounts of these funds to be used to support basic city services. In the second group of cities—Chicago and Los Angeles—fiscal pressure has been less, but there has been considerable discretion in the use of federal dollars, and political conditions include a high level of participation and organization. The cities in the third group—Phoenix, Houston, and Tulsa—are in strong financial condition, have little discretion in what to do with federal money, and have relatively inactive political systems. Thus local officials have a strong incentive to adopt a conservative strategy in dealing with federal grants and to avoid using them to support ongoing city services.

The Politics of Allocation

In the cities classified as hard-pressed, the politics of allocating federal funds have become closely integrated with other forms of local politics. Because federal funds have become a major source of discretionary revenue in the budgets of most of these cities over this period, local officials, particularly mayors and councils, have had a strong incentive to assert control over these funds, both as a source of support for normal city activities and as a potential source of political capital.

This incentive has been strengthened further by the discretion available to these cities in choosing where to spend federal money and by the level of political organization among the constituents of federally supported programs. Because relatively large areas of these cities are eligible to receive federal support, the number of elected officials, particularly council members, with a political stake in the allocation of federal funds has expanded substantially over the last ten years. As Henry Schmandt, George Wendel, and E. Allan Tomey note of St. Louis:

[Earlier] grants—urban renewal, antipoverty, and model cities—were categorical, and the restrictions on their use reduced the opportunity for most aldermen and local politicians to become seriously involved. . . . Only in the case of model cities was the Board of Aldermen in a formal position to influence the distributional process, but relatively few of its members were interested in intervening because the direct benefits of the grant were confined to a small geographical sector of the city. In most cases, only the aldermen in the urban renewal project areas and the model cities neighborhoods were likely to be actively concerned with the disposition of funds. . . . [More recently] the geographical distribution of federal funds. . . , particularly in the case of CDBG, has been the subject of much discussion. . . . Black North Siders complain that the white South Side is favored in the allocation process while community-based organizations in the latter contend that the opposite is true . . . . CDBG has become a battlefield issue in a power struggle between the mayor and the Board of Aldermen.[18]

The constituents of federally supported programs are also well organized and of some political consequence in these cities. All six cities were active participants in the community development and manpower programs of the 1960s. As a result, these functions are not new to city government, and the organizations and departments performing these functions have established stable constituencies with a strong interest in the way federal funds are allocated. In addition, minority and neighborhood groups are well established and organized and are able to press demands for support through normal political channels rather than relying on citizen participation structures attached to the grants themselves.

Not surprisingly, programs supported by federal funds have become major ingredients in mayoral electoral coalitions and means of constituent service by city council members. In Boston, New York, and Detroit, mayors have been the major architects of such federally funded coalitions as well as their principal political beneficiaries. In Boston, for example, Jonathan Katz argues:

The mayor [Kevin White] and the city are committed to providing the social services that depend on federal funds. The political power of the mayor is based to a great extent on the support of recipients of social services, and participants in housing, manpower, and economic development programs. Because civil service and strong unions make the line agencies difficult for the mayor to control, attempts to improve the quality of their services [are] not easy, making a political payoff in this area uncertain. Mayor White has kept his distance from the line agencies . . . choosing instead to devote his time to developing and publicizing the "second level of government" that federal funds have made possible.[19]

A similar use of federal funds to develop and maintain a mayoral electoral coalition was observed in Detroit. As Thomas Anton notes:

[Mayor] Young has seen to it that substantial sums of federal assistance have been poured into neighborhoods, particularly from the community development block grant program. . . . The Community Services Agency and HEW health grants have also been allocated to Detroit neighborhoods. . . . Substantial sums have

18. Henry J. Schmandt, George D. Wendel, and E. Allan Tomey, *Federal Aid to St. Louis* (Brookings Institution, 1983), pp. 43, 47, 50.

19. Jonathan Katz, *The Impact of Federal Grants on the City of Boston* (U.S. Departments of Labor and Commerce, Report MEL 80-15, October 1980), p. 76.

been funneled into neighborhood retail centers, housing, and service improvements all over the city. . . . The city has provided funds to about forty-three neighborhood organizations, including some . . . that have been highly critical of the mayor in past years. . . . With a large and expanding network of neighborhood organizations that have benefited from their interactions with the mayor, a fund of federal money available to nourish this network, and a political style that is enormously popular among a largely black electorate, the mayor has created a base of electoral support that seems secure indeed.[20]

City councils in St. Louis and Cleveland have been particularly active in the allocation of federal funds, especially community development block grants. Mayors have generally been less powerful, both on paper and in practice, in these cities than in Detroit or Boston, allowing councils to assert more control over the allocation of federal funds. In St. Louis, for example, Schmandt, Wendel, and Tomey note that the board of aldermen gained increased control over the allocation of CDBG funds after a conflict over the 1978 application. The board, which had been relatively uninvolved in earlier years, created procedural controls over the expenditure of CDBG funds and forced the reallocation of funds from downtown development, which the mayor had proposed, to neighborhood improvements and housing. The St. Louis authors argue that this initiative was largely the result of constituent pressure:

Initially, such [neighborhood] groups worked through the CDA machinery to obtain funds for their localities. When it became apparent that the Citizen's Advisory Board—and even the CDA commission itself—lacked the power to deliver, community-based organizations began to turn to more traditional politics, pressuring their aldermanic representative to look after neighborhood interests.[21]

In brief, the politics surrounding the allocation of federal money in the cities classified as fiscally hard-pressed are much like other local politics. Involvement by elected officials is substantial, and the constituents of federal funds press demands for funding through much the same channels as for other city services.

A similar pattern appears in Chicago and Los Angeles, but with a slightly different focus. Neither of these places was under severe financial pressure over the period under consideration, and both went to considerable pains to keep federal funds out of basic city services and local funds out of the program areas supported with federal dollars. Like the hard-pressed group of cities, however, both Chicago and Los Angeles have considerable discretion in where they can spend federal money, and both have organized

20. Thomas J. Anton, *Federal Aid to Detroit* (Brookings Institution, 1983), pp. 47–48.
21. Schmandt, Wendel, and Tomey, *St. Louis*, p. 49.

and active political environments in which federal funds are allocated. These two factors have led to the creation of a "federal program arena" independent of the local budgetary process but involving the same decisionmakers and interest groups that are active in other local politics.[22]

The precise nature of this federal arena differs drastically, of course, between these two cities. In Chicago, Charles Orlebeke argues that the actors who allocate federal funds—the mayor and a relatively small set of upper-level city bureaucrats—do so in roughly the same fashion and in response to the same set of political pressures that influence the distribution of other city services:

Although Chicago's political executives have had the most to say about the use of federal aid, they must function within a complex political environment and be sensitive to a variety of competing demands. Chicago politics is a balancing act rather than a dictatorship. Aldermen, ward committeemen, and other functionaries loyal to the machine expect a reasonable cut of all available resources including federal funds; often pitted against the machine are neighborhood groups . . . , citywide civic associations . . . , watch-dog groups . . . , environmentalists . . . , civil rights groups . . . , and public interest lawyers. . . . During the Daley era, the city's executive branch managed both to keep the machine satisfied and to prevent its opponents—sometimes by making concessions—from seriously threatening its hegemony.[23]

Things are different in Los Angeles. Ruth Ross argues that the city's decentralized political system creates strong pressures on each city council member to develop an independent electoral coalition that will keep him or her in office. Community organizations interested in getting federal money are important elements of these coalitions:

The most significant [political] influence of federal programs is the impact of citizen participation requirements in the block grants. . . . As a result of the social funding coming into the city . . . , community groups have gained experience at manipulating power levers. . . . The council grants committee and the full council make final decisions [about the use of federal funds], but these often come after intense lobbying from community groups. . . . [As a result of this lobbying] among the most politically successful programs funded with federal money are those of community groups that draw on both CDBG and CETA. . . . From the point of view of city council members, use of CDBG and CETA money in this way provides constituent programs that are popular with major blocs. At election time, council

---

22. This concept is taken from Pressman, *Federal Programs*.

23. Charles J. Orlebeke, *Federal Aid to Chicago* (Brookings Institution, 1983), pp. 63–64. For a detailed account of the bargaining surrounding the first two years of the CDBG program in Chicago that illustrates this general argument, see Leonard Rubinowitz, "Chicago, Illinois," in Paul R. Dommel, ed., *Decentralizing Urban Policy* (Brookings Institution, 1982).

members can prove they were responsive, but at limited direct cost to the regular city tax base.[24]

The allocation of federal dollars in these cities takes place outside the local budget but not outside the local political system. While these cities face few demands to use federal funds for ongoing city services, they both have substantial discretion in their use of federal funds, and politically important groups put considerable demands on these funds. Under these conditions, federal funds constitute a substantial political resource that local officials have some incentive to control.

In comparison with the first two groups of cities, Houston, Phoenix, and Tulsa separate the allocation of federal dollars from city politics to a much greater degree. Because these cities are in relatively strong financial condition, they have little incentive to use federal funds to subsidize city operations. Further, small areas of these cities are eligible to receive federal funds, minimizing the number of elected officials with a political interest in how federal funds are allocated. Finally, the beneficiaries of federal funds are relatively unorganized, making it difficult for them to press demands through normal political channels. These cities were relatively inactive in the categorical programs of the 1960s, and forms of political organization such as political parties are weak. As a result, city officials have little incentive to involve themselves in decisions about the use of federal funds and have generally ceded control over these dollars to professional staff and concerned private groups.

Susan MacManus notes that in Houston, for example, federally funded programs have been segregated, both financially and politically, from the normal city budget, and their allocation left mostly to program staff:

[The CETA and Community Development] programs were not only fiscally but physically separated from city hall. . . . Their almost total dependence on federal aid stems from the [politically] marginal nature of their functions and the antidependence attitudes of local officials. . . . By and large, Houston's elected officials have played a minor role [in decisions about the use of federal funds] except for making appointments to the various departments and divisions that receive substantial federal aid. . . . Administrators in turn have solicited input from the mayor and various council members, but quietly and privately.[25]

The operation of the allocation process in Tulsa was described by Steve Steib and Lynn Rittenoure in similar terms:

24. Ruth Ross, *The Impact of Federal Grants on the City of Los Angeles* (U.S. Departments of Labor and Commerce, Report MEL 80-21, November 1980), pp. 57, 69, 71.
25. Susan A. MacManus, *Federal Aid to Houston* (Brookings Institution, 1983), pp. 26, 27, 43.

By the time the Board of Commissioners officially acts on the annual budget, few substantive issues remain to be discussed, and the board generally approves the requests. . . . The budget is primarily prepared by specialists in a decentralized format, defended by specialists, and approved by a city commission that has neither the power nor inclination to enforce overall coordination and planning.[26]

In brief, there is substantial variation in the political importance of federal funds in these eleven cities. In cities that have some discretion in deciding how to spend federal dollars and that have politically significant groups interested in their use, elected city officials have had some incentive to gain control of the allocation of these programs and use them as political resources in much the same fashion, and to much the same ends, as other resources. In cities where both discretion and potential political gain have been lacking, officials have directed their attention elsewhere.

The Consequences of Differences in Dependence

There are two main consequences of the difference in the degree of cities' fiscal and political dependence on federal funds. The first is seen in the differing types of services cities have used federal money to support, a variable that should be more closely tied to city fiscal pressure than to city politics. The second is seen in the different ways benefits from federal funds are distributed among income groups, a variable that should be more responsive to variations in local discretion and political conditions.

Functional Use of Federal Funds

For a variety of reasons, cities under fiscal pressure use federal dollars for different purposes (which make them more dependent on federal aid) than more prosperous cities. In particular, hard-pressed cities use substantial amounts of federal money to support ongoing city activities, particularly basic services. More prosperous cities, by contrast, try to avoid using federal funds for these purposes and use them instead in service areas that are not essential to ongoing city operations or that could be terminated without establishing any claim on the city budget.

As table 6 shows, the cities classified as hard-pressed allocated an average

26. Steve B. Steib and R. Lynn Rittenoure, *The Impact of Federal Grants on the City of Tulsa* (U.S. Departments of Labor and Commerce, Report MEL 80-05, March 1980), pp. 56, 57.

Table 6. *Cities' Use of Federal Operating Funds for Basic Services,*
by Financial Condition

City	Percentage of federal funds spent on basic services[a]	Federal spending as percentage of total spending for basic services
Hard-pressed cities		
Detroit	49.0[b]	25.5[b]
St. Louis	49.9[b]	27.0[b]
Cleveland	46.0	24.0
Rochester	92.4	22.3
New York[c]	55.3	22.7
Boston	39.3	13.0
Average	55.3	22.4
More prosperous cities		
Houston	16.5	4.4
Phoenix	30.2	14.7
Tulsa	18.3	11.3
Chicago	28.7	10.9
Los Angeles	10.3	4.5
Average	20.8	9.2

Sources: Same as table 2.
a. Basic services include public safety, public works, sanitation, and general administration. For New York and Boston, schools have also been included. See text for details.
b. Estimated on the basis of employment.
c. Excludes AFDC and medicaid.

of a little over half of federal funds used for operating purposes to support
"basic" services, compared with one-fifth for the more prosperous cities.
Federal funds supported an average of more than 20 percent of city operating expenditures for these services in the hard-pressed places, compared
with less than 10 percent in less distressed cities. Clearly, over this period
at any rate, the hard-pressed cities were more dependent on federal funds
to maintain basic services than were more prosperous cities.

The substantial use of federal funds by the hard-pressed cities to support
basic services appears to reflect explicit decisions to insulate basic service
departments from the consequences of city financial difficulties by using
federal dollars to maintain their operations. In Cleveland, for example,
where federal funds supported more than 25 percent of city spending for
public safety, Richard Tompkins argues:

A charter change in 1968 . . . required that police in Cleveland be paid a wage at
least 3 percent greater than the highest wage paid in other Ohio cities with more
than 50,000 population. . . . Another [reason] was the policy of several city

administrations to insulate the Police Department from personnel layoffs because most political leaders felt that the electorate would not stand for a reduction in police services. As a result of these two factors, Cleveland has relied heavily on multiple sources of federal funds to supplement limited increases in local revenue.[27]

Similar decisions were reported in other cities. For example, Sarah Liebschutz reports that in Rochester growing uncontrollable costs, largely for employee pensions, led local officials to cut local employment by 18 percent between 1973 and 1978. They did so largely by transferring functions to the overlying county government or to private contractors. The only departments exempt from this reduction were police and fire, which have received substantial support from federal funds.

In Detroit, Anton argues, the strength of municipal employee unions, particularly that of the police, has been responsible for city use of federal funds to support basic city services:

Part of the reason that more city jobs were not eliminated has been the strong mutuality of interest between city agencies, reluctant to abandon established service commitments, and municipal employee unions, reluctant to lose jobs. This mutuality of interest, coupled with increasing militance on the part of union leaders faced with an apparently continuous budget "crisis," has achieved very favorable results for city workers . . . imposing significant cost increases on the city even without increases in the number of workers. . . . Federal dollars were used in 1978 to support virtually all city activities: only seven of the forty-five agencies budgeted no federally supported positions in that year. . . . Federal grants supported all of the positions in 1978 for the Departments of Neighborhood Services, Manpower, and Planning. . . . While parks and environmental care . . . were more heavily dependent on federally supported positions than were police, fire, or general administration, federal funding was important for all of these basic city activities.[28]

St. Louis's use of federal funds was shaped by a slightly different set of political factors. The city has no control over its police expenditures, which are set by a state board appointed by the governor, on which the mayor is the only city representative. Because the city is required to support the police department from its own funds at the level set by this board, it has little incentive to use federal funds to support this service. Instead, it has concentrated federal funds heavily in spending on general government and streets, which draw about one-third of their budgets from federal dollars.

In contrast with the hard-pressed cities, the more prosperous cities

27. Richard F. Tompkins and others, *The Impact of Federal Grants on the City of Cleveland* (U.S. Departments of Labor and Commerce, Report MEL 81-19, February 1981), p. 66.

28. Anton, *Detroit*, pp. 30, 32, 33.

adopted relatively explicit policies to minimize the potential consequences to the city budget if federal funds were discontinued. Three such policies can be noted.

The first is to use federal dollars in basic service departments only to support activities that could be easily discontinued if federal dollars were cut. In general, these cities are even less reliant on federal funds to support basic services than the figures in table 6 suggest, since much of the spending these figures reflect supported modest expansions of service or one-time projects, rather than normal operations. Such programs include expansion of street maintenance, police community relations programs, fire surveys, or other activities not directly involved in police patrol or fighting fires. This pattern was particularly marked in the activities supported by public service employment funds. Chicago, for example, used substantial amounts of PSE funds to support basic service departments, but Orlebeke argues that these funds largely supported program expansion:

The city saw PSE . . . as an opportunity to start new programs or expand others, with the federal government picking up most of the tab. For example, the Police Department . . . used federal funds to hire over 100 Spanish-speaking public safety aides. . . . The Fire Department . . . used PSE primarily to develop its elite Mobile Intensive Care Units; CETA funds covered about 200 drivers and attendants eligible for paramedic training, who could move into paramedic vacancies as they occurred.[29]

Los Angeles used PSE funds in similar fashion. Ross notes that PSE funds supported activities that could be terminated without affecting the delivery of services in such departments as public works and traffic:

Even though PSE workers were a significant part of the total work force in these departments, in general they performed functions that could easily be cut back with little harm to basic city services. From the city government's point of view, PSE allowed it to tidy up public facilities, supplement cultural activities, and catch up on the bureaucracy's paper work.[30]

The only exception to this general pattern was Phoenix, which is subject to a state law that limits growth in expenditures financed by local sources but does not apply to expenditures financed by federal grants. John Hall argues that Phoenix budget officials used this loophole to finance a substantial expansion of basic services with federal funds, largely general revenue sharing and PSE funds.

The second major policy followed by more prosperous governments has been to avoid using local money for the activities that federal dollars support,

29. Orlebeke, *Chicago*, p. 35.
30. Ross, *Los Angeles*, p. 39.

thus minimizing potential claims on local dollars if federal funds are discontinued. Most human service activities in these cities are almost totally supported with federal funds. In Tulsa, for example, Steib and Rittenoure note:

City and county departments and trusts contribute a relatively small share in locally raised revenue to social services and to programs that pursue social goals. This situation not only reflects the prevailing sentiment of political leaders, but also is written into the city charter, which states that the city has "no welfare responsibilities." Similarly, city agencies . . . usually use federal money designated for capital improvements in low-income "target" neighborhoods for projects that do not require local agencies to spend money for future operation and upkeep.[31]

Finally, more prosperous governments actively pursue funds from federal capital programs for roads, sewers, subways, and other physical facilities. Although Congress can change authorizations and appropriations for capital programs as readily as for operating programs, capital grants are generally made on a "full funding" basis, under which the federal agency making the grant sets aside the total federal share of a project's cost when the award is made. This practice minimizes the uncertainty associated with federal capital dollars. The more prosperous cities see capital funds as a way to expand services to keep pace with population growth or to enhance economic development without incurring local debt, thereby keeping local taxes down. Federal capital programs accounted for approximately the same share of city capital spending in more prosperous cities as in poor ones in 1978. Spending from federal capital programs was the equivalent of about half of average total capital spending over the previous three years in rich and poor cities alike.[32]

Use of the Economic Stimulus Package

Although in general cities with differing fiscal conditions used federal dollars to support different types of services, this difference did not appear in the use of all federal grants. In particular, cities did not differ appreciably in the ways they spent the largest source of new federal dollars they received in fiscal 1978—the Carter administration's economic stimulus package.

The stimulus package was President Jimmy Carter's response to the lingering effects of the economic recession of 1973–75. Much of the stimulus

31. Steib and Rittenoure, *Tulsa*, pp. 33, 34.
32. U.S. Bureau of the Census, *City Government Finances in 1975–76, 1976–77* (GPO, 1978, 1979); and table 2, col. 4.

spending occurred during fiscal year 1978, which began in October 1977. The primary source of new federal dollars came through two major components of the stimulus package: (1) an expansion of title VI of the public service employment program, designed to provide temporary jobs for those unemployed because of the recession, and (2) the local public works (LPW) program, designed to stimulate employment in the construction industry.[33] Hard-pressed and more prosperous cities used these federal funds in roughly the same ways.

This similarity is particularly marked in the use of PSE funds. During fiscal 1978 the PSE program was funded with money authorized under two titles of the Comprehensive Employment and Training Act: title VI, the countercyclical portion, and title II, which was intended for persons who had been unemployed for long periods. Because title VI was seen as a temporary measure, Congress required localities to use title VI funds for special projects that could be completed within one year. Title VI is often referred to as the "project" portion of PSE. Title II, by contrast, was more permanent and could be used to sustain the levels of public services that governments had been able to provide in the past; this title was thus known as the "sustainment" portion. No matter what their fiscal condition, cities followed similar patterns in their uses of funds under the two PSE titles. Two practices are particularly worthy of note.

First, cities retained a large portion of sustainment positions for assignment to their own government agencies, but assigned large proportions of project positions to other governments or to nonprofit organizations. About two-thirds of all sustainment positions were retained on city payrolls; hard-pressed cities retained more than 80 percent of these positions. With the exception of Cleveland, which was approaching default during this period, fewer than 40 percent of all project slots were retained on city payrolls, and the difference in this regard between hard-pressed and more prosperous cities was small.

Second, both groups of cities used large numbers of project positions either to support social services (largely through subcontracts with com-

---

33. Both these programs were expansions or reauthorizations of already-existing programs, but differed in a number of ways from earlier versions. For descriptions of these differences in LPW, see U.S. Commerce Department, Economic Development Administration, *Local Public Works Program: Status Report* (GPO, 1978). For a more complete description of the PSE program, see Richard P. Nathan and others, *Public Service Employment: A Field Evaluation* (Brookings Institution, 1981). The third part of the stimulus package, the antirecession fiscal assistance program, is not considered here because several of the more prosperous places received only negligible allocations, making comparisons difficult.

munity organizations) or to expand such activities as park maintenance and street cleaning, which could use relatively unskilled workers who could be put to work quickly. Some cities used project funds to rehire some laid-off city workers, but such uses were significantly less common than under the sustainment title.

These uses of project funds had two roots. First, it was simply harder to use project funds than sustainment funds to support normal operations. The eligibility requirements for hiring were more restrictive than those under the sustainment portion, and there was a one-year limit on the length of time an individual could occupy a project position. There was no such limit for sustainment positions. Finally, there was an informal requirement that one-third of all project slots be subcontracted to community organizations; no such requirement was attached to sustainment funds.

Second, project funds were not likely to continue. The stimulus package—which expanded the project portion more than the sustainment portion—was presented publicly as a one-time infusion of funds rather than as a permanent new program, and there was considerable public speculation that the project PSE funds might be made part of the Carter administration's welfare reform program. Governments thus had little incentive to use project funds to support normal operations.

This incentive was weakened further by the relative improvement in the financial condition of most of the hard-pressed cities between 1976, when local economies were still affected by the 1973–75 recession, and 1977, when most had recovered. Both Detroit and Boston, for example, moved from general fund revenue deficiences in 1976 to revenue excesses in 1977, and New York's revenue deficiency was more than $100 million lower in 1977 than in 1976.[34]

There were more substantial differences between hard-pressed and more prosperous cities in the use of local public works funds. LPW was a more significant portion of the capital budgets of harder-pressed cities than of less distressed ones. On the average, among the hard-pressed cities studied, LPW allocations received during 1978 accounted for 21 percent of an average year's capital spending (calculated from figures for the previous three years). The comparable figure was 13 percent in the more prosperous places.

Hard-pressed cities also used LPW funds more frequently to support

34. For a detailed assessment of the financial conditions of these cities over this period, see Philip M. Dearborn, *The Financial Health of Major U.S. Cities in 1977* (Boston: First Boston Corporation, 1978).

renovation and rehabilitation. Typical LPW projects in poorer cities were relatively small ones, such as street and sidewalk reconstruction and repair or renovation of public facilities, that had been postponed in the past because of financial problems. In several cities, the backlog of such projects had grown considerably as a result of earlier reductions in borrowing and maintenance expenditures. In Boston, for example,

Part of the success in launching the LPW program can be attributed to the abundance of already planned capital projects that had been delayed for lack of funds. The requirement that LPW projects have workers on the job in 90 days precluded the funding of any new projects. . . . However, the requirement actually suited the city's situation, because many capital projects were on the shelf, most having the necessary design work and approvals in place. These projects had been passed over in the CDBG budget and in the capital budget, which earlier had been curtailed because of fiscal constraints. [35]

Attempts to link LPW funds with other economic development efforts appear to have been more the exception than the rule, even though during this period several cities were undertaking substantial downtown redevelopment campaigns, which LPW could have been used to support. Only in Detroit and Chicago were substantial amounts of LPW funds successfully plugged into ongoing economic development efforts, particularly downtown projects. Cleveland also tried to use LPW funds as a part of larger plans for downtown development, but had considerable legal and political difficulties in implementing these plans. In other cities, the program's emphasis on projects that could be started quickly, a maximum limit on federal support for any single project, and an emphasis by planning agencies on projects that would create large numbers of jobs led cities to tilt project selection toward smaller ones that could be begun relatively quickly and to look for other funding for larger projects. [36] Thus Ross reports the following in Los Angeles:

When LPW was passed, the city submitted 212 projects from its backlog of second-priority capital improvement projects. The federal government funded thirty-four in round 1 for $26.5 million. . . . When round 2 regulations were amended to permit the city to select projects, a top priority was the Piper Technical Center. The city wanted to concentrate the money, but the Economic Development Administration . . . wanted projects that could be completed more rapidly and rejected it. . . . The city set up a nonprofit corporation to build the technical

35. Katz, *Boston*, p. 34.

36. LPW funds were granted in two rounds, the first in winter 1977 and the second in fall 1977. In the first, the Economic Development Administration selected projects from applications submitted by local governments. In the second round, local governments were allowed to choose projects to be funded from applications already on file.

center. The council members then chose from the remaining projects based on their districts' needs. Most members essentially conducted a round robin, selecting one project per district until the money was allocated.[37]

In sum, several factors reduced the incentive of cities to attempt to use PSE funds to support normal city operations or to integrate LPW funds with larger economic development efforts. These factors included federal agency pressures to obligate and spend large amounts of money in a short period of time, program features designed to increase the rate at which funds were spent, uncertainty about future funding, and short-term improvements in cities' fiscal condition. Dependence on stimulus funds, even among the hard-pressed cities, was generally far less than on other federal dollars.

Distribution of Benefits from Federal Funds

Because grant dollars have subsidized general operations in harder-pressed cities and the politics surrounding the allocation of these dollars have been more intense, the benefits from federally funded programs have been more broadly dispersed there than in the more prosperous cities, where benefits have been more concentrated among lower-income groups. These differences in benefits have been particularly marked in CDBG and CETA. These block grants were intended to provide services to lower-income groups, but were also meant to give local governments substantial discretion in how to use the funds.

Table 7 presents estimates of the percentage of expenditures from CDBG, the PSE portion of CETA, and all federal funds that benefited low- and moderate-income groups in each city in 1978. Benefits from federal programs were allocated in a number of ways. The benefits from capital projects, such as those funded by CDBG or LPW funds, were allocated on the basis of the income of the area where the projects were located. The income incidence of service programs such as PSE or child nutrition was determined by the characteristics of the recipients. The benefits from such programs as downtown development or general revenue sharing, which can be said to benefit the population as a whole, were allocated on the basis of the proportion of each income group in the total population. The figures in the table should be viewed as approximations, but they do provide a rough indication of which groups were the primary beneficiaries of federal funds.

37. Ross, *Los Angeles*, pp. 36–37.

Table 7. *Estimated Percentage of Federal Grant Expenditures
Benefiting Low- and Moderate-Income Groups, 1978*[a]

City	Community development block grants[b]	Public service employment[c]	All federal grants
Hard-pressed cities			
Detroit	47	32	59
Cleveland	35	33	55
Rochester	68	82	62
Boston	30	81	n.a.
St. Louis	37	91	76
Average	43	64	63
More prosperous cities			
Phoenix	93	85	88
Los Angeles	52	100	91
Tulsa	54	100	52
Chicago	76	100	73
Average	69	96	76

Sources: Same as table 2.

a. Income groups are defined by reference to 1970 city median family income. "Low income" indicates income less than 50 percent of city median; "moderate income" indicates income between 50 and 80 percent of city median. Comparable data were not available for New York or Houston.

b. Benefits defined by income composition of the area where activities supported by CDBG funds were located. Data were generally drawn from local applications for funds and hence reflect planned rather than actual expenditures.

c. Benefits defined by characteristics of individuals paid with PSE funds.

On average, low- and moderate-income groups were the primary beneficiaries of more than three-quarters of federally supported expenditures in more prosperous cities, compared with about three-fifths of such expenditures in harder-pressed cities. The share of CDBG and PSE expenditures that benefited lower-income groups in the more prosperous cities was almost one and one-half times larger than in the poorer ones. Lower-income groups in the more prosperous cities were the beneficiaries of over 69 percent of CDBG expenditures, compared with less than 50 percent in the hard-pressed cities. The disparity in the income levels of PSE participants was even greater. Almost 100 percent of PSE participants were members of lower-income groups in more prosperous cities, compared with less than two-thirds in hard-pressed cities.

This disparity in the beneficiaries of federal funds in the two groups of cities can be traced to several sources, most of which have already been discussed. First, the hard-pressed cities had more discretion in spending federal dollars. They were less constrained by CDBG regulations, and it was relatively easy for them to convert sustainment PSE funds into a source of support for general city activities. Second, because they were unable to support ongoing city services at politically acceptable levels from local revenue, they had a considerable incentive to use federal funds to support these services, which benefit the entire city population. Officials in these cities also had a considerable incentive to use these funds as political resources, which led them to spread benefits around, rather than focusing them in the poorest areas of the city.

The politics of this spreading process varied among cities. In New York, Boston, and Detroit, mayors used federal funds as a way to develop and maintain political support. Julia Vitullo-Martin argues that New York's tendency to spread the benefits occurred as a result of two factors. One was increased demands on these funds from middle-income areas, accentuated by a city charter that mandates formal citizen participation in the allocation of funds. The second was administrative pressure to implement programs quickly, which tends to favor programs benefiting moderate- and middle-income areas. She argues further that the ability to allocate funds to a wide range of areas strengthened the mayor's position in responding to these demands:

Federal funds help the mayor out, because he controls the money and can distribute CDBG and employment money and contracts to the boroughs. There's enough poverty and dilapidated housing to go around, so the mayor can easily choose to favor some boroughs and neighborhoods over others, without in any way violating federal regs. At the same time, he can always call on federal regs to justify denying aid to others.[38]

Katz argues that Boston has followed a more explicit strategy of dispersing funds as widely as possible:

In distributing the services and jobs funded by federal aid programs, city officials try to provide "something for everyone." Many decisions on how to allocate federal funds concentrate on spending something in each of the city's neighborhoods. Because the city's largest political constituency is its middle-income residents, officials make sure they obtain some benefits. . . . Under this distributive strategy, growing numbers of city residents are receiving services and expect them to continue. There are obvious political benefits for an administration to pursue this policy which actively reaches out to a broader constituency.[39]

By contrast, pressures for spreading funds in Cleveland and St. Louis came largely from the city council and were centered around community development funds. In Cleveland, Tompkins argues, social service agencies and mayors as well as the council saw the potential political benefits of

38. Julia Vitullo-Martin, "The Impact of Federal Grants on New York City, FY 1972–FY 1978" (n.p., May 1981), p. 91.
39. Katz, Boston, p. 81.

spreading federal funds. Council members sought benefits for their wards; social service agencies sought funds to support their activities; mayors wanted federal funds to support normal citywide operations. As a result of these common interests, almost 75 percent of the city was defined as eligible for community development projects. This area was narrowed to 40 percent in 1978 as a result of pressure from HUD, community groups, and the community development director, but Tompkins argues that the pressures from the council for dispersal of funds remained substantial:

Despite these efforts, almost half of the 1979 CDBG expenditures were for services dispersed throughout the city such as public safety, environmental health, and programs delivered by nonprofit social service agencies. Programs targeted toward neighborhoods continued to be subject to three council reviews and the accompanying political considerations.[40]

The major form of spreading the benefits of PSE funds has been their use to rehire laid-off city workers, as was done extensively in New York, Cleveland, and Detroit. New York, for example, rehired approximately 2,500 policemen, sanitation, and park workers by using PSE funds, while Detroit rehired several hundred policemen.

The richer cities are more complex. In Phoenix, Houston, and Tulsa, as noted earlier, there was relatively little incentive to spread federal dollars for any reason. Because these cities have little discretion in where to spend federal money, fewer elected officials are in a position to claim political credit for its uses. Similarly, there is little incentive to use federal funds as a source of support for normal city operations. These conditions have strengthened the bargaining position of program staff and others interested in targeting funds to lower-income areas. Hall argues that in Phoenix, for example, the concentration of federal funds in South Phoenix was the result of both local political conditions and federal pressure:

A local coalition concerned about the general deterioration of the area and particularly its housing problems has, until recently, been successful in selling CDBG as an act designed to benefit low- and moderate-income individuals. HUD has reinforced this interpretation by rejecting plans for parks and recreational facilities in more affluent parts of the city. . . . Although current CDBG and [other social agency] targeting appear[s] to stem from combined federal incentives and local politics, other targeting efforts are much more the direct result of federal formulas and regulations.[41]

In Chicago and Los Angeles, the situation has been more complicated, particularly with regard to CDBG. Because federal programs are important

40. Tompkins and others, *Cleveland*, p. 62.
41. Hall, *Phoenix*, pp. 61, 64.

political resources in these cities, the politics surrounding their allocation have been more complex than in cities where decisions about federal money are largely left to staff. In Chicago, the city government's desire to disperse federal funds to as many neighborhoods as possible has conflicted with demands from neighborhood groups and the constituencies of the former model cities and community action agencies, who have been pushing the city to target funds. The situation has been further complicated by the political and legal maneuvering surrounding the implementation of the *Gautreaux* decision, in which a federal judge in 1969 ordered the city to locate subsidized housing outside minority areas. Orlebeke argues that these forces together have compelled the city to concentrate an increasing amount of funds in low-income areas:

The city government and HUD have groped for an accommodation with each other, and with the city's contending political forces. [The attorney for the *Gautreaux* plaintiffs] and his allies submit detailed "administrative complaints" to HUD each year charging noncompliance with the city's housing assistance goals; neighborhood groups also go to HUD directly to complain. . . . HUD has been very reluctant, however, to intervene in the local CDBG planning process, or to punish the city by cutting CDBG funds. The result is that the city's CDBG planners maneuver and negotiate among neighborhood groups, civil rights organizations, social service agencies, and other interests in order to fashion the program each year. Although HUD may sometimes issue stern admonitions, in the end it has generally backed whatever plan the city finally comes up with. . . . It does appear, however, that the combination of HUD pressure, political demands from neighborhood groups, and prevailing current wisdom in urban planning, not necessarily in that order of importance, have moved Chicago's community development program toward the targeting objective.[42]

In Los Angeles, the main effect of political maneuvering around CDBG has been to produce a greater spreading of funds among income groups than in other prosperous cities. The city has no single clearly identifiable pocket of poverty within which funds have to be spent, and the city's decentralized political system encourages council members to pursue federal funds as a means of maintaining voter support.

Unless the federal government requires otherwise, the legislators prefer to split all federal grants fifteen ways. . . . Most council members have learned the political benefits of federal grants, especially the CDBG and LPW programs. These programs enable council members to provide visible public improvements and social services for their constituents at relatively little cost to the city's own treasury. . . . After the bargaining among members is over, almost every member gets some funds, regardless of whether the member's district has a large proportion of low- and

42. Orlebeke, *Chicago*, pp. 61, 72, 73.

moderate-income residents or not. In the first four years of the CDBG program, every council district received at least some money, although the districts with the lowest median income received the largest amounts of CDBG aid.[43]

Conclusion

This analysis has identified three distinct patterns in federal aid's budgetary and political impact among the eleven cities under consideration. In the six cities that have been classified as financially hard-pressed, as having broad discretion in their use of federal funds, and as having a high level of political activity and organization (Boston, Cleveland, Detroit, New York, Rochester, and St. Louis), federal funds have become a major source of support for basic, ongoing city services; the funds have been allocated through regular political channels; elected officials (rather than program staff) have controlled the allocation of these funds; and the benefits have tended to be widely distributed among income groups.

In the two cities that have been classified as less hard-pressed financially but still having broad discretion in the use of federal funds and a high level of political activity (Chicago and Los Angeles), federal funds have been used primarily for secondary services or for basic services in ways that could be easily discontinued. Otherwise, their style of allocation, control of allocation by elected officials, and distribution of benefits is similar to the six hard-pressed cities.

In the three cities that have been classified as more prosperous, however (Houston, Phoenix, and Tulsa), all the factors differ from the other eight cities. They have had little discretion in their use of federal funds, their level of political activity is low, federal funds have been used almost totally for secondary services and have been allocated outside political channels by program staff (rather than elected officials), and benefits have been distributed primarily to lower-income groups.

Three further points are particularly worthy of note. First, the amount of federal money a city receives—whether compared with its own revenues or judged against any other standard—has little relation to its dependence on these funds to support ongoing city services. Hard-pressed and more prosperous cities have used federal funds to support very different activities, but these differences are not reflected in the amount of federal money

43. Ross, *Los Angeles*, pp. 1, 56.

these two kinds of cities receive. According to the figures in table 3, the cities classified as prosperous are, on average, more dependent on federal money than the hard-pressed cities, because the federal aid they receive is larger relative to local taxes than the comparable figure for the hard-pressed cities.

Second, there is considerable variety in the politics surrounding the allocation of federal funds, and these different political conditions appear to influence the way federal aid is spent. In cities where elected officials are the major decisionmakers, federal funds are more likely to be used to support basic services and to benefit the population at large than in places where professional staff control the allocation of federal money. The presumption made by more formal models—that federal money is allocated more or less the same in all cities and in response to the same set of forces that drive the allocation of local funds—appears unwarranted, at least for this set of cities. Politics differ, and they cause spending patterns to differ as well.

Finally, the conditions surrounding grants, particularly the uncertainty of their continuation and the amount of discretion they provide local officials, appear to have a considerable effect on how cities spend federal dollars. In spite of the large amounts of money provided to these cities under the economic stimulus package, for example, both the uncertainty of continued support and federal agency pressure to spend money in particular ways appear to have led all but the most hard-pressed of these cities to avoid using these funds to support ongoing city activities. In similar fashion, different degrees of discretion stemming from CDBG regulations appear to have produced different uses of these funds across these cities.[44]

The differences in dependence and in the politics surrounding the allocation of federal funds suggest that substantial reductions in grant programs will have a very different impact on these cities. The next section suggests some of these differences.

The Consequences of Cuts

The case studies reported on in this paper dealt with the local political and budgetary response to a massive buildup in the level of federal grants

---

44. For a more developed version of these latter two arguments, see V. Lane Rawlins and Richard P. Nathan, "The Field Network Evaluation Studies of Intergovernmental Grants: A Contrast with the Orthodox Economic Approach," *American Economic Review*, vol. 72 (May 1982, *Papers and Proceedings, 1981*), pp. 98–102.

to cities that occurred in the mid-1970s. In particular, these studies focused on federal aid received and spent during 1978, which marked the high point of federal urban support as a percentage of both federal outlays and local revenue.

Since 1978 the federal aid picture for cities has changed sharply. The Carter administration's attempt to make the economic stimulus package programs permanent was unsuccessful, and substantial restrictions were imposed on hiring under the PSE program.[45] As a result of these and other changes, the amount of federal support for cities leveled off between 1978 and 1982. More recently, and more important, major changes in the level and form of urban aid have been initiated by the Reagan administration. These changes fall into three major categories.

The first and most important has been a major reduction in funding for a number of grant programs. The Reagan administration's 1982 budget, the most successful to date in reducing grant spending, abolished the PSE program entirely, significantly restricted eligibility and benefits for a number of income security programs, and reduced funding for urban development action grants, mass transit construction and operation, airport and sewer construction, employment and training, and most education programs. As a result of these changes, total grant spending declined from $94.7 billion in 1981 to $88.1 billion in 1982. This spending decline was most pronounced in grants that support services and other operating programs by state and local governments. Federal spending for these programs declined by $6 billion, or over 20 percent, between 1981 and 1982. By contrast, capital grant spending declined by less than 10 percent over this same period (although more substantial declines were projected for later years), while welfare spending actually increased slightly.[46]

Subsequent attempts by the Reagan administration to reduce grant spending further have been less successful. Congress has become less willing to authorize additional cuts in domestic spending, and the recent recession produced significant increases in spending for most income security programs. The recession also led to the adoption of the Surface

45. For a more detailed description of these changes, see Nathan and others, *Public Service Employment*, pp. 118–19.

46. *Special Analyses, Budget of the United States Government, Fiscal Year 1985*, table H-8. For detailed descriptions of the changes enacted in the 1982 budget, see John William Ellwood, ed., *Reductions in U.S. Domestic Spending: How They Affect State and Local Governments* (Transaction Books, 1982); and John L. Palmer and Isabel V. Sawhill, eds., *The Reagan Experiment* (Washington, D.C.: Urban Institute, 1982).

Transportation Assistance Act of 1981 and the Emergency Jobs Creation Act of 1982, both designed to reduce unemployment by increasing spending on a variety of grant programs, primarily for the construction or rehabilitation of sewers, roads, and other public facilities. These recession-related changes have produced projections that total grant spending will increase to $102 billion by 1985, an increase of 15.9 percent since 1982.[47]

While welfare and capital grant spending has increased in response to the recession, federal spending for operating programs has remained at its depressed 1982 level. Although congressional sentiment has become less disposed toward reducing spending for domestic programs, there has been little support to date for permanent restoration of appropriations that were cut in such program areas as employment and training, social services, or education. The Emergency Jobs Creation Act of 1982 increased funding for a number of operating programs, but in most cases this increase was for only one year and did not completely replace the earlier cuts in these programs. Spending for these programs is expected to increase by more than $2 billion between 1982 and 1984, but even this enhanced level is $5.5 billion, or 16 percent, less than spending in 1980.[48] Once the temporary increase in funding for these programs expires, funding will decline further.

The second major change in the grant system stemming from Reagan administration initiatives has been the consolidation of a number of relatively small categorical programs into block grants to state governments, generally with a substantial reduction in funds. The 1982 budget folded fifty-seven categorical programs in the areas of community development, health, education, community and social services, and energy assistance into nine such grants with total budget authority of about $7.2 billion annually, a reduction of approximately 25 percent. Subsequent budgets have proposed further consolidation, but with less success. The training titles of the CETA program were replaced in 1982 by the Job Training Partnership Act, which is administered by state governments, and several mass transit programs were consolidated, but further proposals to consolidate programs in education, child welfare, and welfare administration were unsuccessful.

The most radical change in the grant system proposed by the Reagan administration has been two attempts to "turn back" control of a number of grant programs to state and local governments. The 1983 budget proposed

47. *Special Analyses*, table H-8.
48. Ibid.

a major restructuring of the grant system that would have turned back some 125 programs with annual outlays of approximately $40 billion, including all urban aid programs, to state governments. This proposal would also have swapped responsibility for several income security programs by providing for complete federal financing of the medicaid program in exchange for state assumption of funding of the programs for aid to families with dependent children and food stamps.[49] The 1984 budget contained a less radical proposal for providing state and local governments with more control over how federal funds are spent. The administration proposed the consolidation of several programs with annual outlays of approximately $18 billion. State and local governments would have been provided with increasing authority over a five-year period to use these funds as they saw fit.[50] Neither proposal attracted support from Congress or state officials, and the Reagan administration did not actively press for their enactment.

The most substantial immediate consequence of Reagan administration initiatives for state and local governments, in short, has been an appreciable reduction in the level of federal support for operating programs that provide services of various types, largely health, social services, and education. While spending for income support programs has been reduced compared with what it would have been under earlier rules, this change creates no immediate pressure on state and local budgets. Since state and local governments are required to pay an appreciable fraction of the costs of most income security programs, federal reductions in eligibility or benefits for these programs may save these governments substantial funds. While some former clients of federally supported welfare programs may subsequently receive support from state-financed general assistance programs, the level of benefits under these programs is unlikely to be as large as the state's share of benefits under the federally supported programs.

Although a complete description of the consequences of these changes in federal operating revenue is obviously beyond the scope of this essay, there is sufficient information available on the impact of the Reagan cuts in cities to provide at least a partial extension of the model already advanced.

49. For a description and critique of this proposal, see Edward M. Gramlich and Deborah S. Laren, "The New Federalism," in Joseph A. Pechman, ed., *Setting National Priorities* (Brookings Institution, 1982).

50. For a description of this proposal, see Rochelle Stanfield, "Revised New Federalism Plan Would Do Little to Change Power, Authority," *National Journal*, vol. 16 (March 5, 1983), pp. 487, 518–19.

This evidence is drawn from a major study of the consequences of the Reagan domestic program currently under way at the Princeton Urban and Regional Research Center.[51]

The model presented here suggests that the local response to reductions in federal aid of the type and magnitude contained in recent budgets should largely be determined by the city's financial condition and the political strength of the beneficiaries of the federal programs being affected. In cities that have relatively few financial problems, the major effect of reductions in grant dollars should be to reduce the level of local spending on social and other secondary services. As discussed earlier, local officials in these cities have used substantial amounts of federal money to support these services and the activities of community groups as a way of insulating themselves from potential claims on local resources if federal funds were discontinued. Since program beneficiaries in these cities are generally unorganized and have limited ability to press claims on local officials to continue activities previously supported by federal dollars, it should be expected that cuts in federal funds in these cities will be translated fairly directly into reductions in services.

In harder-pressed cities, expectations are more complex. These cities have used federal funds to support basic services that are much harder to discontinue than more politically peripheral activities, and federal program beneficiaries are better organized and more able to press claims on elected officials than those in more prosperous places. Thus it might be expected that local politicians will be under considerable pressure to continue at least a portion of the activities supported by federal dollars by using local funds. On the other hand, because of these cities' financial difficulties, elected officials may not be in a position to respond to more than a small fraction of these demands. Officials in these cities would probably attempt to dedicate whatever local resources are available to replacing federal funds that supported basic services, but beneficiaries of human services programs may have sufficient political strength to compel at least partial replacement of federal funds in other areas. Under these circumstances, local officials may be required to seek increases in local taxes, reduce basic service levels, or do both.

51. The results of this study are reported in Richard P. Nathan, Fred C. Doolittle, and associates, *The Consequences of Cuts: The Effects of the Reagan Domestic Program on State and Local Governments* (Princeton Urban and Regional Research Center, 1983); and Ellwood, ed., *Reductions in U.S. Domestic Spending*. New York and Detroit are not included in this study.

While detailed evidence is not yet at hand, available information is broadly consistent with this argument. The major consequence of the reductions in federal aid in more prosperous places appears to have been a decline in the level of secondary services, while several of the harder-pressed cities appear to have reduced the level of basic services as well. This pattern is particularly marked in these cities' response to elimination of the public service employment program, which was the most substantial reduction experienced by most of these cities over this period.

Elimination of Public Service Employment

In the more prosperous cities, the effects of eliminating PSE appear to have been negligible. Most of these cities had protected themselves against such an eventuality by subcontracting substantial numbers of PSE positions and concentrating these funds in services that could be easily terminated without establishing any claim on the city budget. As noted earlier, Congress imposed considerable restrictions on PSE hiring practices in 1978. Most of the prosperous places appear to have begun reducing their involvement in the program at this time by reducing the number of PSE positions in their own agencies and moving former PSE workers they wished to retain onto the city payroll. Phoenix, for example, moved approximately 500 positions from PSE to city funding well before the program was eliminated, and Chicago shifted more than 350 slots.

Hard-pressed cities were hurt more by the PSE termination. Because of their fiscal position, these cities had been unable to reduce their participation in the program after the 1978 restrictions took effect. They were compelled either to seek waivers of program requirements or to continue participation under the more stringent regulations.

Boston, Rochester, and St. Louis were forced to reduce basic services after PSE ended. All three cities had come under increased fiscal pressure since 1978—Rochester as a result of a court-mandated rollback of property tax rates, and Boston and St. Louis as a result of major tax limitation measures. All were in the process of reducing city-funded work forces when PSE was terminated. As the St. Louis authors note:

[The elimination of PSE], involving a loss of $21 million to St. Louis, is a severe blow because of the city's heavy reliance on PSE workers to supplement its regular civil service complement (which itself has now been significantly reduced). . . . The reduction in federal aid comes at a particularly inopportune time because of the climate created by the nationwide tax resistance movement. . . . Confronted with a threatened initiative referendum to abolish the 10 percent utility tax, the Board of Aldermen in 1979 passed a law phasing out the levy on residential users by 1983. When fully in effect the repeal will reduce tax revenues by about $24 million a year.[52]

Detroit and Cleveland, by contrast, were able to avoid major layoffs when PSE ended by securing large increases in local income tax rates. While the Cleveland increase passed relatively easily, the Detroit increase was the result of a long, complex, and bitterly contested campaign. State legislative approval was required to place the increase on the ballot. The legislature gave its approval, but required the city to secure substantial wage concessions from city employees and to sell city bonds to eliminate a $120 million deficit. The city was able to meet all conditions, but only after a major lobbying effort.

This argument is reinforced by an examination of employment patterns in these two groups of cities over this period. Between 1978 and 1981, basic service employment in the cities classified here as relatively prosperous increased or declined only slightly; employment in secondary services declined substantially. With the exception of Houston, where employment in both basic and secondary services grew by more than 30 percent over this period, employment in secondary services declined by an average of over 11 percent; employment in basic services, on the average, increased slightly. By contrast, in the cities classified here as hard-pressed, employment in basic services declined by an average of almost 8 percent.[53] New York City, which had laid off large numbers of police officers, fire fighters, and other basic service workers through the mid-1970s following its near default in 1975, was the only hard-pressed city that increased the number of basic service employees on its payroll over this period. While these changes in employment obviously cannot be attributed entirely to the loss of PSE, it appears reasonable to conclude that the strategy pursued by the more prosperous places of using federal funds for secondary services was largely successful, while harder-pressed cities experienced substantially greater difficulties in coping with the loss of these funds.

Cuts in Other Programs

The difference between more and less prosperous cities was much less pronounced in their response to cuts in other federal programs. With the

52. Schmandt, Wendel, and Tomey, *St. Louis*, p. 66.
53. Calculations from U.S. Bureau of the Census, *City Government Employment* (GE series, no. 2), various issues.

exception of Houston, which continued a variety of federally supported programs by using city revenue, neither rich nor poor cities replaced federal revenue with local funds to any appreciable degree. Although a variety of small projects were continued and replacement was more frequent in overlying governments such as counties and school districts, there was little systematic attempt in either hard-pressed or more prosperous places to continue federally supported programs from local sources.[54] There are several reasons for this limited replacement.

First, and perhaps most important, is a general worsening of the financial condition of both local and state governments over this period, even among those localities classified here as relatively prosperous. As a variety of observers have noted, the overall financial condition of the state and local sector has worsened appreciably since 1980. In addition to coping with reductions in federal aid, state and local officials have also had to deal with the adverse financial consequences of persistently high rates of unemployment—which have produced both significant declines in revenue and equally significant increases in service loads for income support and other social service programs—and with the effects of a variety of tax and expenditure limitation measures enacted during recent years. As a result of these financial problems, many local and, especially, state governments have been compelled to take relatively drastic measures to cut services, increase taxes, or do both.[55]

This general decline was also apparent among the cities under consideration here. While conditions worsened most appreciably in the harder-pressed places, most of the cities classified here as more prosperous also experienced significant deterioration in their financial positions. Los Angeles, for example, lost several million dollars in state "bail-out" funds that it had been receiving since the passage of Proposition 13 in 1978.[56]

A worsening financial condition militates against replacement of federally supported programs in several ways. First, it strengthens the bargaining

54. For evidence and detailed discussion, see Nathan, Doolittle, and associates, *The Consequences of Cuts*, chaps. 4, 7.

55. For surveys of state and local government financial condition over this period, see Deborah Matz and John Petersen, "Trends in the Fiscal Conditions of Cities: 1980–1982," prepared for the Joint Economic Committee, 97 Cong. 2 sess. (GPO, 1982); National Governors Association–National Association of State Budget Officers, "Fiscal Survey of the States, 1983" (Washington, D.C.: NGA–NASBO, 1983); and George E. Peterson, "The State and Local Sector," in Palmer and Sawhill, eds., *The Reagan Experiment*. pp. 157–217.

56. For details, see Nathan, Doolittle, and associates, *The Consequences of Cuts*, pp. 122–43.

position of local officials who wish to avoid committing local funds to replace lost federal money. State or local financial difficulties may also serve to weaken the demands from federal program beneficiaries to replace losses in federal funds with local revenue. Groups or agencies affected by federal cuts may see themselves as having less chance of success in securing local funds than if these funds were more readily available and hence may be less likely to make attempts to convince local governments to replace lost federal revenue. Further, if these beneficiaries also receive services or support financed by state or local revenue, they may deem it more important to focus their lobbying efforts on protecting these funds rather than on replacing lost federal dollars. Neighborhood groups, for example, might be more likely to attempt to prevent police layoffs or attempts to close local schools rather than to try to maintain federally supported social programs providing services to their area.

A second reason for the limited use of local funds to continue federally supported programs is the loosening of federal restrictions in some programs, which allowed local governments to continue politically popular activities by distributing federal funds rather than committing local revenue. The program most frequently used as a source of funds in this fashion has been the community development block grant program. As part of a general campaign to reduce federal red tape and control over local use of grant funds, Reagan appointees in the Department of Housing and Urban Development repealed regulations requiring funds to be spent on activities that primarily benefited low- and moderate-income groups and substantially broadened the types of activities that CDBG funds could be used to support.[57] This increased discretion allowed cities to replace cuts in other federal programs with CDBG funds rather than using local revenue. Among the cities under consideration here, approximately half, split evenly between more and less prosperous places, used appreciable amounts of CDBG funds to restore cuts in other federal programs.

A final reason for the similarity of response between rich and poor cities to these program reductions lies in the nature of the cuts themselves. Unlike the PSE program, which had relatively few restrictions on the types

57. For a general description of the Reagan administration's deregulation efforts, see Catherine Lovell, "Effects of Regulatory Changes on States and Localities," in ibid., pp. 169–87. For a description of the changes in the CDBG program, see Michael Rich, "Fiscal and Political Implications of the New Federalism: An Assessment of the CDBG Experience in 10 Cities," paper prepared for the 1983 annual meeting of the Midwest Political Science Association.

of services that could be funded and allowed for waivers of those restrictions, most of the other programs that were reduced more closely restricted the types of services and the income groups that could benefit. Typically, most funded the provision of what have been labeled here as secondary services—health, job training, social services, and housing—to lower-income groups. Furthermore, many of these programs, particularly those consolidated into the block grants, were administered by state or federal agencies with relatively little involvement by local officials.

Considering the factors argued earlier to be influential in local decisions about federal funds, both hard-pressed and more prosperous cities should have responded to these programs in roughly the same way and should have reacted in roughly the same fashion to reductions in their funding. Since these programs provided little discretion in what they could be used to support and which groups could benefit, local officials, even in hard-pressed cities, had little incentive to view them as potential sources of either revenue or political capital. Unlike PSE, where elected officials in hard-pressed cities developed considerable financial and political stakes in program operation, these programs provided little opportunity either to use funds to support normal city activity or to garner political credit by intervening in their operation. Operations in both rich and poor cities alike have been determined largely by program staff with relatively little involvement from elected officials. In neither case did elected officials see themselves as having any stake in the continuation of these programs.

As a result, the local response to cuts in these programs has been similar in both sets of cities. Local restoration of federal cuts is largely determined by the political saliency of the service being cut and the ability of program beneficiaries and providers to convince elected officials that their interest will be served by continuing the program. Most successful in having cuts at least partially restored from either local or federal funds were such activities as health and day care, which have well-organized and politically active provider groups, as opposed to such activities as job training and social services, whose "producer" groups are less well organized.[58]

The local response to federal aid cuts largely follows the pattern suggested by the model of grant allocations advanced earlier in this essay. In financially hard-pressed cities, certain federal grants became important political resources for local officials and important sources of revenue for ongoing

---

58. See Nathan, Doolittle, and associates, *The Consequences of Cuts*, chap. 7, for a detailed statement of this argument.

services. In these cities, cuts in these politically important programs have resulted either in significant cuts in the level of basic city services or substantial local tax increases. In more prosperous places, and in programs which are less important politically, program cuts have largely been translated into reductions in the level of secondary services, with continuation of funding being determined mainly by the political strength of service providers and the availability of alternative federal sources of funding.

Index

Adams, Charles F., Jr., 2n, 34n
Advisory Commission on Intergovernmental Relations, 74
Aid to families with dependent children (AFDC), 23, 33, 50, 112, 156
Allen, James, 80
Anderson, Martin, 71n
Anton, Thomas, 135, 141

Bahl, Roy, 109n, 111n
Bailey, Stephen K., 9n, 76
Banfield, Edward C., 56n, 69
Beer, Samuel H., 54n, 57n, 64n, 67n, 100
Block grants: and Carter, 45; and categorical grants, 19, 20; and community development, 38, 89, 101; and devolution, 56, 59–60, 76, 89, 99; education, 104–05; and Ford, 30, 98–99; health, 18–19, 105; and Nixon, 26, 28, 57; and Reagan, 49, 104, 106, 155. See also Community development block grants
Brown, Lawrence D., 3, 99n
Burchell, Robert, 111n
Burke, Vee, 73n
Burke, Vincent J., 73n

CAA. See Community action agencies
Cahill, William, 20
Calkins, Susannah E., 56n, 57n, 68n, 94
CAP. See Community action programs
Caputo, David A., 57n
Carter, Jimmy: and categorical grants, 43; and changes in federal funding, 43–45, 51; and community development block grants, 38–39, 116; and economic stimulus, 36–37, 120, 143–45, 154; and grant design, 36–37, 52; and manpower block grants, 37, 99–100; and revenue sharing, 44, 49; and

urban policy, 39–43, 52, 130
Categorical grants: and block grants, 19, 20; and Carter, 43; and cities, 109, 138; and community development block grants, 95; consolidation of, 55, 56–57, 73; and devolution, 60–61, 65, 73–74, 93; education programs, 81–84; and Ford, 30; and Johnson, 17, 18, 22; and Nixon, 26, 78; and Reagan, 47, 104, 106, 155; rural programs, 78–81. See also Grants-in-aid
CDBG. See Community development block grants
CETA. See Comprehensive Employment and Training Act of 1973
Cities: and cuts in federal aid, 111, 154–58, 161–63; decisionmaking in allocating federal aid, 121, 125, 126, 130, 132, 134–39; dependence on federal aid, 110–14, 121–24, 134, 152–53; discretion in use of federal aid, 130–31, 134, 136–37, 153; distribution of federal benefits, 147–52, 153; federal regulation and, 97, 115–16, 117, 130, 161; financial condition of, 125–29, 152–53, 160–61, 162; grants to during 1970s, 31, 108–10; level of political organization in, 131–33; politics of federal aid to, 114–15, 116–18, 134–39; uncertainty of funding levels for, 115–16, 117, 124, 126, 153; use of federal aid for basic services, 112–14, 119, 120–21, 122–24, 125, 134, 139–43, 147, 152–53, 157–58. See also Local government
Clark, Jane Perry, 54n
Clay, Henry, 55
Cleaveland, Frederick N., 11n
Cohen, Michael, 126n
Cohen, Richard E., 104
Coleman, James S., 75, 83

Cole, Richard L., 57n, 101n
Community action agencies (CAAs), 14, 25, 69, 109
Community action programs (CAPs), 90, 91
Community development block grants (CDBG), 27, 56, 57, 58, 94, 98, 103, 161; and Carter, 38, 116; and cities, 109, 113, 116, 117, 119, 130, 131, 135–38, 153; and devolution, 56, 71, 72, 87–90, 91–92, 95, 96–97, 101; distribution of benefits of, 147–52; and Ford, 30, 116; and Reagan, 116, 161. *See also* Block grants
Comprehensive Employment and Training Act of 1973 (CETA), 27–28, 33, 50, 52, 56, 57, 58, 94, 144, 155; and Carter, 36, 37, 45, 100–01; and cities, 113, 117, 137, 138, 142; as devolution success, 70, 72, 91–92, 93, 95, 97; and Ford, 99; and Nixon, 103. *See also* Job Training Partnership Act; Public service employment
Congress: and community development, 87–90, 94; and cuts in federal aid, 154–56; and devolution politics, 58, 77–84, 93, 103, 106; and Economic Development Administration, 41; and energy assistance, 45, 104; and grant design, 30, 56–57; and housing, 12, 14, 72; and Johnson, 6; and public service employment, 115, 158; and Reagan, 47, 51, 53, 102, 103, 104; and revenue-sharing measures, 26–27, 44, 78–86, 100; and urban renewal, 12–13
Conlon, Timothy J., 55n, 57n, 78n
Countercyclical grants, 34, 36–37, 42
Courant, Paul, 114n
Crime Control Act of 1973, 28
Cronin, Thomas E., 84n

Davidson, Roger H., 57n, 70n
Davis, Otto A., 62n
Dearborn, Philip M., 129n, 145n
Decentralization, 56, 63, 66, 68; and devolution politics, 59–60, 72; and Nixon, 25–26, 68, 97; and Reagan, 50, 102, 155–56
Demonstration Cities and Metropolitan Development Act of 1966 (model cities), 13–15, 16, 71–72
Department of Commerce, 37, 48
Department of Health, Education, and Welfare (HEW), 33, 135
Department of Housing and Urban Development (HUD), 11–12, 27, 38–39, 97, 151, 161; and Congress, 12, 14, 72; and Johnson, 11–12. *See also* Community development block grants; Housing; Urban policy
Department of Labor, 28
Dependence on federal aid: levels of, 133–34; measuring, 110–11, 121–24; redefining, 111–14
Derthick, Martha, 26n, 33n, 61n, 64n, 99n
de Tocqueville, Alexis, 59n, 64n
Devolution measures: and American federalism, 54–55, 63–66; and Carter, 99, 100; and Ford, 98–99, 100; and Nixon, 3, 56–57; normative context of, 59–63; proponents of, 66–67; and Reagan, 99–100, 101–07; strategy for, 93–98, 104–07; structural variables of, 78–93, 102–04; and values, 68–77, 102
Dirksen, Everett, 20
Dommel, Paul R., 2n, 36n, 38n, 39n, 57n, 66n, 96n, 97n, 100n, 101n, 112n, 137n
Doolittle, Fred C., 47n, 157n, 160n, 162n

Economic Development Administration (EDA), 41
Economic Opportunity Act of 1964, 10
Elementary and Secondary Education Act (ESEA): and Carter, 45; as devolution failure, 75–76, 81–84; and Johnson, 8–9, 20–21; and Reagan, 48, 104–05
Ellwood, John William, 154n, 157n
Emergency Employment Act, 33
Emergency Jobs Creation Act of 1982, 155
Employment. *See* Comprehensive Employment and Training Act of 1973; Emergency Employment Act; Emergency Jobs Creation Act of 1982; Job Corps; Job Training Partnership Act; Public service employment
Energy assistance grants, 45
ESEA. *See* Elementary and Secondary Education Act

Federal government: coordination with states, 17–18, 23, 25; and devolution, 59–63; and New Federalism, 24–26; and special districts, 16. *See also* Cities; Local government; Revenue sharing; State government
Federal Water Pollution Control Act Amendments, 33, 48
Finn, Chester E., 75n
Fiscal assistance, 41–42, 56, 73. *See also* Revenue sharing
Food stamps: and Johnson, 10–11, 61; and Nixon, 24, 33; and Reagan, 50, 156
Ford, Gerald, 2, 21, 35, 43, 98–99, 100, 116
Ford, William, 81n
Formula grants: to cities, 109; defined, 16–17; and Nixon, 36
Fossett, James W., 3
Friedman, Milton, 62n

Galchick, Janet, 127n
Gautreaux decision, 151
General Services Administration, 42
Gibson, Kenneth, 90
Glaser, William A., 64n
Goodall, Leonard, 133n
Gousha, Richard, 82
Gramlich, Edward M., 114n, 156n
Grants-in-aid: allocation of, 109, 114, 130,
   134–39; and Carter administration, 35–45,
   51–52, 99–100; cuts in, 46–49, 106, 110–
   11, 117, 153–63; design of, 15–17, 21, 26–
   31, 36, 49–50; discretion in use of, 56, 60–
   61, 130–31, 134, 136–37, 152, 153; distribution of benefits of, 147–52; expansion of,
   3, 6, 7, 31, 43–45, 54–56, 108; functional
   use of, 139–43; and Johnson administration, 6–21, 51–52; measuring city dependence on, 110–14, 121–24; and Nixon-Ford
   administrations, 21–35, 51–52, 67–68, 73,
   74, 78, 99–100, 102–03; and Reagan administration, 46–51, 52–53, 101–07, 154–58;
   as source of city revenue, 108, 115, 121–
   24. *See also* Block grants; Categorical grants;
   Countercyclical grants; Formula grants;
   Project grants
Graves, W. Brooke, 55n
Great Society, 6–7, 21–22, 69, 74
Grodzins, Morton, 55n

Haar, Charles M., 13n
Hall, John, 131, 132–33, 142, 150
Handicapped, defined, 10
Harris, Patricia, 39
Health, and Reagan, 105. *See also* Medicaid;
   Medicare; Partnership for Health Act of
   1966
Health insurance, national, 62
Heidenheimer, Arnold J., 65n
HEW. *See* Department of Health, Educa-
   tion, and Welfare
Hill-Burton Act, 11
Housing: and Carter, 45; and Johnson, 12–
   13; and Reagan, 49. *See also* Community
   development block grants; Department of
   Housing and Urban Development
Housing Act of *1949*, 12
Housing and Community Development Act,
   27, 38, 56
Housing and Urban Development Act of *1965*,
   12
HUD. *See* Department of Housing and Ur-
   ban Development
Humphrey, Hubert, 78, 80

Jackson, John E., 62n
Jefferson, Thomas, 59n
Job Corps, 10, 92
Job Training Partnership Act (JTPA), 47, 49–
   50, 155
Johnson, Lyndon B.: and design of grants,
   15–21, 25, 28, 51–52; and growth of grant
   programs, 2, 5, 6–11, 31, 43, 51; urban
   emphasis of programs, 11–15
JTPA. *See* Job Training Partnership Act
Jump, Bernard, Jr., 111n
Juvenile Justice and Delinquency Prevention
   Act of *1974*, 44

Katz, Jonathan, 135, 146n, 149
Kennedy, John F., 8, 10, 11–12, 61, 69
Kennedy, Robert, 22
Kestnbaum Commission, 55
Key, V. O., Jr., 54n, 66n
Kleindienst, Richard, 85

Laird, Melvin, 18, 22–23, 55–56
Laren, Deborah S., 156n
Larkey, Patrick D., 114n
Law Enforcement Assistance Administration
   (LEAA), 44, 76, 99; as devolution failure,
   84–86
Leman, Christopher, 65n
Levitan, Sar A., 70n
Liebschutz, Sarah F., 2n, 141
Listokin, David, 111n
Local government: and devolution, 54, 55,
   56, 88–90, 93; and federalism, 61, 63–66;
   financial condition of, 160–61; and New
   Federalism, 29–31; and Reagan, 46, 155–
   56; and revenue sharing, 26–29, 34, 35,
   73, 100. *See also* Cities; Revenue sharing;
   State government
Local public works (LPW), 37, 144, 145–47,
   151
Long, Norton, 73n
Lovell, Catherine, 161n

McClellan, John, 84
MacManus, Susan A., 2n, 138
Mangum, Garth L., 70n
Manpower Development and Training Act of
   1962, 90
Manpower programs: and devolution, 70, 90–
   92, 95; and Johnson, 9–10; and Nixon, 23
March, James, 126n
Matz, Deborah, 160n
Mayhew, David R., 77n
Medicaid, 7–8, 45, 49, 50, 63, 112
Medicare, 7, 62
Meeds, Lloyd, 81, 82

Mergit, Astrid, 110n
Mieszkowski, Peter, 114n
Mills, Wilbur, 26, 74, 87, 94
Mirengoff, William, 115n
Model cities. *See* Demonstration Cities and
  Metropolitan Development Act of *1966*
Monagan, John S., 84
Moneypenny, Phillip, 61n
Mosher, Edith K., 9n, 76
Moynihan, Daniel P., 21n, 69n, 73n, 75
Munger, Frank, 66n
Murphy, Jerome T., 76n
Muskie, Edmund S., 17

Nathan, Richard P., 2n, 4n, 10n, 24n, 27n,
  34n, 36n, 47n, 56n, 57n, 68n, 94, 96n,
  109n, 112n, 115n, 116n, 144n, 153n, 154n,
  157n, 160n, 162n; and block grants, 106;
  and federalism, 54–55
National Housing and Urban Development
  Act of *1968*, 72
National School Lunch Act of *1946*, 11
Neighborhood Youth Corps, 10
New Federalism: elements of, 23–24; federal
  and state functions in, 24–26; origins and
  aims of, 21–23; and Reagan, 50–53; and
  revenue sharing, 73
Nixon, Richard M., 102, 104; and devolution,
  56, 67–68, 97; and grant design, 26–31, 51,
  91; and growth of grant programs, 31–35,
  43; and New Federalism, 21–26, 51, 102–
  03; and revenue sharing, 57, 73–74, 78,
  81, 94, 100
Nutrition programs: and Carter, 45; and Ford,
  30; and Johnson, 10–11; and Reagan, 49

Oakland, William, 114n
Office of Economic Opportunity (OEO), 14,
  23, 102
Office of Management and Budget, 42–43
Olson, Johan P., 126n
Omnibus Crime Control and Safe Streets Act
  of *1968*, 19–20
Orfield, Gary, 57n, 81n
Orlebeke, Charles J., 2n, 137, 142, 151

Palmer, John L., 154n, 160n
Palmer, Kenneth T., 2, 4, 23n
Parris, Judith H., 11n
Partnership for Health Act of *1966*, 18, 19,
  99
Pechman, Joseph A., 36n, 112n, 156n
Pell, Claiborne, 105n
Perkins, Carl, 81
Petersen, John, 111n, 160n
Peterson, George E., 52n, 160n

Policy Group on Urban and Regional De-
  velopment, 39–40
Pollingue, Mary L., 59n
Poverty, 61–62. *See also* War on Poverty
Pressman, Jeffrey, 132n, 137n
Prewitt, Kenneth, 132n
Price, Douglas, 66n
Princeton Urban and Regional Research Cen-
  ter, 157
Project grants, 16–17, 36
Proposition *13*, 43
PSE. *See* Public service employment
Public Health Act, 18
Public service employment (PSE), 117, 120;
  abolishment of, 154, 158–59; distribution
  of benefits, 147–48, 150; use of funds to
  support basic services, 115, 126–27, 142,
  144–45, 147, 150. *See also* Comprehensive
  Employment and Training Act of *1973*
Public Works and Economic Development
  Act of *1965*, 41
Public works programs, 37, 145–46, 147, 151

Rawlins, V. Lane, 153n
Reagan, Michael D., 57n, 96
Reagan, Ronald: and community development block grants, 116, 161; and devolution, 4, 101–07; and federal grant cuts, 46–
  49, 154–58; and grant design, 49–50; and
  medicare, 62n; and "new federalism," 50–
  53
Regulation, cities and, 115–16, 117, 130
Reichley, A. James, 55
Revenue sharing, 29, 34, 58, 59, 60, 109; and
  Carter, 44, 99; and community develop-
  ment, 87–90; as devolution success, 69,
  73–74, 87, 94, 96; and education, 81–84;
  and law enforcement, 84–86; and Nixon,
  26–27, 56–57, 94, 98; and Reagan, 103–04;
  and rural development, 78–81
Rich, Michael, 161n
Rittenoure, R. Lynn, 138–39, 143
Rodino, Peter, 84, 86
Ross, Ruth, 137–38, 142, 146, 152n
Rubinfeld, Daniel, 114n
Rubinowitz, Leonard, 137n
Rural development, 78–81
Rural Development Act of *1972*, 28, 81

Sanzone, John G., 57n
Sawhill, Isabel V., 154n, 160n
Schlesinger, Arthur M., Jr., 60n
Schmandt, Henry J., 2n, 134, 136, 159n
Schroeder, Larry, 111n
Seiberling, John, 86
Shultz, George, 70

Sindler, Allan P., 76n, 84n
Stafford, Robert, 105
Stanfield, Rochelle L., 43n, 104n, 105n, 156n
Stanton, James, 86
State and Local Fiscal Assistance Act, 26–27, 56, 73. *See also* Revenue sharing
State government: aid to cities, 111; and devolution, 54, 55, 56, 93, 95; expansion of, 23; federal government coordination with, 17–18, 23, 25; and federalism, 61, 63–66; financial condition of, 160; and New Federalism, 24–25; and Reagan, 46, 50, 155–56. *See also* Cities; Local government; Revenue sharing
Steib, Steve B., 138–39, 143
Strange, John H., 69n
Sundquist, James L., 14n, 61n
Supplemental fiscal assistance, 41–42
Surface Transportation Assistance Act of 1981, 154–55. *See also* Transportation
Syed, Anwar, 59n

Tomey, E. Allan, 2n, 134n, 136, 159n
Tompkins, Richard F., 141n, 149–50
Transfer payments, 24, 30, 47, 49
Transportation: and Carter, 45; as devolution failure, 76; and Johnson, 6; and Reagan, 48, 154–55

UDAG. *See* Urban development action grants

Unemployment, 9–10, 33, 34–35, 120, 144, 155. *See also* Comprehensive Employment and Training Act of 1973; Emergency Employment Act; Emergency Jobs Creation Act of 1982; Job Corps; Job Training Partnership Act; Public service employment
Unemployment compensation, 24
Unions, municipal employee, 141
Urban development action grants (UDAGs), 38–39
Urban policy: and Carter, 39–43; and devolution, 70–72, 87–90; and Johnson, 11–15; and Nixon-Ford, 31. *See also* Cities

Vitullo-Martin, Julia, 149
Vocational education, 10, 92
Vocational Rehabilitation Act, 10

Walker, David B., 104n
War on Poverty, 22, 24. *See also* Poverty
Waste treatment works, 33–34
Wastewater treatment plants, 47–48
Weaver, Robert, 12
Weicker, Lowell, 105
Wendel, George D., 2n, 134, 136, 159n
White, Kevin, 135
Wilson, James Q., 99n
Wright, Deil S., 56n